Computer Programming Languages

Computer Programming Languages

Gordon Hurley

www.willfordpress.com

Published by Willford Press,
118-35 Queens Blvd., Suite 400,
Forest Hills, NY 11375, USA

ISBN: 978-1-64728-024-6

Cataloging-in-Publication Data

Computer programming languages / Gordon Hurley.
p. cm.
Includes bibliographical references and index.
ISBN 978-1-64728-024-6
1. Programming languages (Electronic computers). 2. Electronic data processing.
3. Languages, Artificial. I. Hurley, Gordon.
QA76.7 .C66 2022
005.13--dc23

For information on all Willford Press publications
visit our website at www.willfordpress.com

Contents

Preface

A programming language is a formal language which is made up of a set of instructions to derive different kinds of output. Algorithms are implemented in computer programming using programming languages. A programming language is often described as comprising of two components, namely syntax and semantics. The form is specified by the syntax while semantics deals with the meaning of the programming language. Semantics is further subdivided into static semantics and dynamic semantics. The way in which a programming language classifies expressions and values into types is defined using a type system. A programming language has a finite and precise definition and thus can be described in its entirety. They are generally developed by using a higher level of abstraction in order to increase the problem solving capability. The various sub-fields of programming languages along with technological progress that have future implications are glanced at in this book. It presents this complex subject in the most comprehensible and easy to understand language. This textbook will serve as a valuable source of reference for graduate and post graduate students.

A detailed account of the significant topics covered in this book is provided below:

Chapter 1- The set of rules as well as the vocabulary which is used to instruct a computing device for performing specific tasks is known as a programming language. Some of the high level programming languages are C++, Java and PHP. This is an introductory chapter which will introduce briefly all the significant aspects of computer programming languages.

Chapter 2- There are a number of important components in a programming language. A few of them are variables, arrays, functions, characters, loops and syntax diagrams. This chapter has been carefully written to provide an easy understanding of the varied facets of these components of programming languages.

Chapter 3- C++ is the name of a general purpose programming language which is an extension of the C programming language. The topics elaborated in this chapter will help in gaining a better perspective about C++ as well as the different variables, functions, arrays and pointers in it.

Chapter 4- Hypertext Markup Language refers to the standard markup language which is used for documents that are designed to be displayed in a web browser. One of the most popular versions of hypertext markup language is HTML5. All the diverse principles of HTML5 as well as its applications have been carefully analyzed in this chapter.

Chapter 5- JavaScript refers to a high-level, interpreted scripting language which conforms to the ECMAScript specification. It can support functional, imperative and event-driven programming styles. Some of the popular JavaScript frameworks are AngularJS, ReactJS, MeteorJS and jQuery. The diverse applications of these JavaScript frameworks have been thoroughly discussed in this chapter.

Chapter 6- Python is the name of a high-level, interpreted, general-purpose programming language. Its design philosophy stresses on code readability. Some of the common python GUI frameworks are PyQt, Tkinter and PyGtk. The chapter closely examines these key frameworks of Python as well as its advantages to provide an extensive understanding of the subject.

It gives me an immense pleasure to thank our entire team for their efforts. Finally in the end, I would like to thank my family and colleagues who have been a great source of inspiration and support.

Gordon Hurley

Introduction to Computer Programming Language

The set of rules as well as the vocabulary which is used to instruct a computing device for performing specific tasks is known as a programming language. Some of the high level programming languages are C++, Java and PHP. This is an introductory chapter which will introduce briefly all the significant aspects of computer programming languages.

A programming language is a set of commands, instructions, and other syntax use to create a software program. Languages that programmers use to write code are called "high-level languages." This code can be compiled into a "low-level language," which is recognized directly by the computer hardware.

High-level languages are designed to be easy to read and understand. This allows programmers to write source code in a natural fashion, using logical words and symbols. For example, reserved words like function, while, if, and else are used in most major programming languages. Symbols like <, >, ==, and != are common operators. Many high-level languages are similar enough that programmers can easily understand source code written in multiple languages.

Examples of high-level languages include C++, Java, Perl, and PHP. Languages like C++ and Java are called "compiled languages" since the source code must first be compiled in order to run. Languages like Perl and PHP are called "interpreted languages" since the source code can be run through an interpreter without being compiled. Generally, compiled languages are used to create software applications, while interpreted languages are used for running scripts, such as those used to generate content for dynamic websites.

Low-level languages include assembly and machine languages. An assembly language contains a list of basic instructions and is much more difficult to read than a high-level language. In rare cases, a programmer may decide to code a basic program in an assembly language to ensure it operates as efficiently as possible. An assembler can be used to translate the assembly code into machine code. The machine code, or machine language, contains a series of binary codes that are understood directly by a computer's CPU. Needless to say, machine language is not designed to be human readable.

Language Types

Machine and Assembly Languages

A machine language consists of the numeric codes for the operations that a particular computer can execute directly. The codes are strings of 0s and 1s, or binary digits ("bits"), which are frequently converted both from and to hexadecimal (base 16) for human viewing and modification. Machine language instructions typically use some bits to represent operations, such as addition, and some to represent operands, or perhaps the location of the next instruction. Machine language is difficult to read and write, since it does not resemble conventional mathematical notation or human language, and its codes vary from computer to computer.

Assembly language is one level above machine language. It uses short mnemonic codes for instructions and allows the programmer to introduce names for blocks of memory that hold data. One might thus write "add pay, total" instead of "0110101100101000" for an instruction that adds two numbers.

Assembly language is designed to be easily translated into machine language. Although blocks of data may be referred to by name instead of by their machine addresses, assembly language does not provide more sophisticated means of organizing complex information. Like machine language, assembly language requires detailed knowledge of internal computer architecture. It is useful when such details are important, as in programming a computer to interact with input/output devices (printers, scanners, storage devices, and so forth).

Business-oriented Languages

COBOL

COBOL (common business oriented language) has been heavily used by businesses since its inception in 1959. A committee of computer manufacturers and users and U.S. government organizations established CODASYL (Committee on Data Systems and Languages) to develop and oversee the language standard in order to ensure its portability across diverse systems.

COBOL uses an English-like notation—novel when introduced. Business computations organize and manipulate large quantities of data, and COBOL introduced the record data structure for such tasks. A record clusters heterogeneous data such as a name, ID number, age, and address into a single unit. This contrasts with scientific languages, in which homogeneous arrays of numbers are common. Records are an important example of "chunking" data into a single object, and they appear in nearly all modern languages.

SQL

SQL (structured query language) is a language for specifying the organization of databases (collections of records). Databases organized with SQL are called relational because SQL provides the ability to query a database for information that falls in a given relation. For example, a query might be "find all records with both last_name Smith and city New York." Commercial database programs commonly use a SQL-like language for their queries.

Education-oriented Languages

BASIC

BASIC (beginner's all-purpose symbolic instruction code) was designed at Dartmouth College by John Kemeny and Thomas Kurtz. It was intended to be easy to learn by novices, particularly non-computer science majors, and to run well on a time-sharing computer with many users. It had simple data structures and notation and it was interpreted: a BASIC program was translated line-by-line and executed as it was translated, which made it easy to locate programming errors.

Its small size and simplicity also made BASIC a popular language for early personal computers. Its recent forms have adopted many of the data and control structures of other contemporary languages, which makes it more powerful but less convenient for beginners.

Pascal

About 1970 Niklaus Wirth of Switzerland designed Pascal to teach structured programming, which emphasized the orderly use of conditional and loop control structures without GOTO statements. Although Pascal resembled ALGOL in notation, it provided the ability to define data types with which to organize complex information, a feature beyond the capabilities of ALGOL as well as FORTRAN and COBOL. User-defined data types allowed the programmer to introduce names for complex data, which the language translator could then check for correct usage before running a program.

During the late 1970s and '80s, Pascal was one of the most widely used languages for programming instruction. It was available on nearly all computers, and, because of its familiarity, clarity, and security, it was used for production software as well as for education.

Logo

Logo originated in the late 1960s as a simplified LISP dialect for education; Seymour Paper and others used it at MIT to teach mathematical thinking to schoolchildren. It had a more conventional syntax than LISP and featured "turtle graphics," a simple method for generating computer graphics. (The name came from an early project to program a turtle like robot.) Turtle graphics used body-centred instructions, in which an object was moved around a screen by commands, such as "left 90" and "forward," that specified actions relative to the current position and orientation of the object rather than in terms of a fixed framework. Together with recursive routines, this technique made it easy to program intricate and attractive patterns.

Hypertalk

Hypertalk was designed as "programming for the rest of us" by Bill Atkinson for Apple's Macintosh. Using a simple English-like syntax, Hypertalk enabled anyone to combine text, graphics, and audio quickly into "linked stacks" that could be navigated by clicking with a mouse on standard buttons supplied by the program. Hypertalk was particularly popular among educators in the 1980s and early '90s for classroom multimedia presentations. Although Hypertalk had many features of object-oriented languages, Apple did not develop it for other computer platforms and let it languish; as Apple's market share declined in the 1990s, a new cross-platform way of displaying multimedia left Hypertalk all but obsolete.

Object-oriented Languages

Object-oriented languages help to manage complexity in large programs. Objects package data and the operations on them so that only the operations are publicly accessible and internal details of the data structures are hidden. This information hiding made large-scale programming easier by allowing a programmer to think about each part of the program in isolation. In addition, objects may be derived from more general ones, "inheriting" their capabilities. Such an object hierarchy made it possible to define specialized objects without repeating all that is in the more general ones.

Object-oriented programming began with the Simula language, which added information hiding to ALGOL. Another influential object-oriented language was Smalltalk, in which a program was a set of objects that interacted by sending messages to one another.

C++

The C++ language, developed by Bjarne Stroustrup at AT&T in the mid-1980s, extended C by adding objects to it while preserving the efficiency of C programs. It has been one of the most important languages for both education and industrial programming. Large parts of many operating systems, such as the Microsoft Corporation's Windows 98, were written in C++.

Ada

Ada was named for Augusta Ada King, countess of Lovelace, who was an assistant to the 19th-century English inventor Charles Babbage, and is sometimes called the first computer programmer. Ada, the language, was developed in the early 1980s for the U.S. Department of Defense for large-scale programming. It combined Pascal-like notation with the ability to package operations and data into independent modules. Its first form, Ada 83, was not fully object-oriented, but the subsequent Ada 95 provided objects and the ability to construct hierarchies of them. While no longer mandated for use in work for the Department of Defense, Ada remains an effective language for engineering large programs.

Java

In the early 1990s, Java was designed by Sun Microsystems, Inc., as a programming language for the World Wide Web (WWW). Although it resembled C++ in appearance, it was fully object-oriented. In particular, Java dispensed with lower-level features, including the ability to manipulate data addresses, a capability that is neither desirable nor useful in programs for distributed systems. In order to be portable, Java programs are translated by a Java Virtual Machine specific to each computer platform, which then executes the Java program. In addition to adding interactive capabilities to the Internet through Web "applets," Java has been widely used for programming small and portable devices, such as mobile telephones.

Visual Basic

Visual Basic was developed by Microsoft to extend the capabilities of BASIC by adding objects and "event-driven" programming: buttons, menus, and other elements of graphical user interfaces (GUIs). Visual Basic can also be used within other Microsoft software to program small routines.

Declarative Languages

Declarative languages, also called non-procedural or very high level, are programming languages in which (ideally) a program specifies what is to be done rather than how to do it. In such languages there is less difference between the specification of a program and its implementation than in the procedural languages described so far. The two common kinds of declarative languages are logic and functional languages.

Logic programming languages, of which PROLOG (programming in logic) is the best known, state a program as a set of logical relations (e.g., a grandparent is the parent of a parent of someone). Such languages are similar to the SQL database language. A program is executed by an "inference engine" that answers a query by searching these relations systematically to make inferences that will answer a query. PROLOG has been used extensively in natural language processing and other AI programs.

Functional languages have a mathematical style. A functional program is constructed by applying functions to arguments. Functional languages, such as LISP, ML, and Haskell, are used as research tools in language development, in automated mathematical theorem provers, and in some commercial projects.

Scripting Languages

Scripting languages are sometimes called Little languages. They are intended to solve relatively small programming problems that do not require the overhead of data declarations and other features needed to make large programs manageable. Scripting languages are used for writing operating system utilities, for special-purpose file-manipulation programs, and, because they are easy to learn, sometimes for considerably larger programs.

PERL (practical extraction and report language) was developed in the late 1980s, originally for use with the UNIX operating system. It was intended to have all the capabilities of earlier scripting languages. PERL provided many ways to state common operations and thereby allowed a programmer to adopt any convenient style. In the 1990s it became popular as a system-programming tool, both for small utility programs and for prototypes of larger ones.

Document Formatting Languages

Document formatting languages specify the organization of printed text and graphics. They fall into several classes: text formatting notation that can serve the same functions as a word processing program, page description languages that are interpreted by a printing device and most generally, markup languages that describe the intended function of portions of a document.

TeX

Text formatting systems, unlike WYSIWYG ("What You See Is What You Get") word processors, embed plain text formatting commands in a document, which are then interpreted by the language processor to produce a formatted document for display or printing. TeX marks italic text, for example, as which is then displayed as this is italicized.

TeX largely replaced earlier text formatting languages. Its powerful and flexible abilities gave an expert precise control over such things as the choice of fonts, layout of tables, mathematical notation, and the inclusion of graphics within a document. It is generally used with the aid of "macro" packages that define simple commands for common operations, such as starting a new paragraph; LaTeX is a widely used package. TeX contains numerous standard "style sheets" for different types of documents, and these may be further adapted by each user. There are also related programs such as BibTeX, which manages bibliographies and has style sheets for all of the common bibliography styles, and versions of TeX for languages with various alphabets.

PostScript

PostScript is a page-description language developed in the early 1980s by Adobe Systems Incorporated on the basis of work at Xerox PARC. Such languages describe documents in terms that can be interpreted by a personal computer to display the document on its screen or by a microprocessor in a printer or a typesetting device.

PostScript commands can, for example, precisely position text, in various fonts and sizes, draw images that are mathematically described, and specify colour or shading. PostScript uses postfix, also called reverse Polish notation, in which an operation name follows its arguments. Thus, "300 600 20 270 arc stroke" means: draw (stroke) a 270-degree arc with radius 20 at location (300, 600). Although PostScript can be read and written by a programmer, it is normally produced by text formatting programs, word processors, or graphic display tools.

The success of PostScript is due to its specification's being in the public domain and to its being a good match for high-resolution laser printers. It has influenced the development of printing fonts, and manufacturers produce a large variety of PostScript fonts.

SGML

SGML (standard generalized markup language) is an international standard for the definition of markup languages; that is, it is a Meta language. Markup consists of notations called tags that specify the function of a piece of text or how it is to be displayed. SGML emphasizes descriptive markup, in which a tag might be "<emphasis>." Such a markup denotes the document function, and it could be interpreted as reverse video on a computer screen, underlining by a typewriter, or italics in typeset text.

SGML is used to specify DTDs (document type definitions). A DTD defines a kind of document, such as a report, by specifying what elements must appear in the document—e.g., <Title>—and giving rules for the use of document elements, such as that a paragraph may appear within a table entry but a table may not appear within a paragraph. A marked-up text may be analyzed by a parsing program to determine if it conforms to a DTD. Another program may read the markups to prepare an index or to translate the document into PostScript for printing. Yet another might generate large type or audio for readers with visual or hearing disabilities.

World Wide Web Display Languages

HTML

The World Wide Web is a system for displaying text, graphics, and audio retrieved over the Internet on a computer monitor. Each retrieval unit is known as a Web page, and such pages frequently contain "links" that allow related pages to be retrieved. HTML (hypertext markup language) is the markup language for encoding Web pages. It was designed by Tim Berners-Lee at the CERN nuclear physics laboratory in Switzerland during the 1980s and is defined by an SGML DTD. HTML markup tags specify document elements such as headings, paragraphs, and tables. They mark up a document for display by a computer program known as a Web browser. The browser interprets the tags, displaying the headings, paragraphs, and tables in a layout that is adapted to the screen size and fonts available to it.

XML

HTML does not allow one to define new text elements; that is, it is not extensible. XML (extensible markup language) is a simplified form of SGML intended for documents that are published on the Web. Like SGML, XML uses DTDs to define document types and the meanings of tags used in them. XML adopts conventions that make it easy to parse, such as that document entities are marked by both a beginning and an ending tag, such as <BEGIN>..........</BEGIN>. XML provides more kinds of hypertext links than HTML, such as bidirectional links and links relative to a document subsection.

Because an author may define new tags, an XML DTD must also contain rules that instruct a Web browser how to interpret them—how an entity is to be displayed or how it is to generate an action such as preparing an e-mail message.

Web Scripting

Web pages marked up with HTML or XML are largely static documents. Web scripting can add information to a page as a reader uses it or let the reader enter information that may, for example, be passed on to the order department of an online business. CGI (common gateway interface) provides one mechanism; it transmits requests and responses between the reader's Web browser and the Web server that provides the page. The CGI component on the server contains small programs called scripts that take information from the browser system or provide it for display. A simple script might ask the reader's name, determine the Internet address of the system that the reader uses, and print a greeting. Scripts may be written in any programming language, but, because they are generally simple text-processing routines, scripting languages like PERL are particularly appropriate.

Another approach is to use a language designed for Web scripts to be executed by the browser. JavaScript is one such language, designed by the Netscape Communications Corp., which may be used with both Netscape's and Microsoft's browsers. JavaScript is a simple language, quite different from Java. A JavaScript program may be embedded in a Web page with the HTML tag <script language="JavaScript">. JavaScript instructions following that tag will be executed by the browser when the page is selected. In order to speed up display of dynamic (interactive) pages, JavaScript is often combined with XML or some other language for exchanging information between the server and the client's browser. In particular, the XMLHttpRequest command enables asynchronous data requests from the server without requiring the server to resend the entire Web page. This approach, or "philosophy," of programming is called Ajax (asynchronous JavaScript and XML).

VB Script is a subset of Visual Basic. Originally developed for Microsoft's Office suite of programs, it was later used for Web scripting as well. Its capabilities are similar to those of JavaScript, and it may be embedded in HTML in the same fashion.

Behind the use of such scripting languages for Web programming lies the idea of component programming, in which programs are constructed by combining independent previously written components without any further language processing. JavaScript and VB Script programs were designed as components that may be attached to Web browsers to control how they display information.

Elements of Programming

Despite notational differences, contemporary computer languages provide many of the same programming structures. These include basic control structures and data structures. The former provide the means to express algorithms, and the latter provide ways to organize information.

Control Structures

Programs written in procedural languages, the most common kind, are like recipes, having lists of ingredients and step-by-step instructions for using them. The three basic control structures in virtually every procedural language are:

- Sequence—Combine the liquid ingredients, and next add the dry ones.

- Conditional—If the tomatoes are fresh then simmer them, but if canned, skip this step.

- Iterative—Beat the egg whites until they form soft peaks.

Sequence is the default control structure; instructions are executed one after another. They might, for example, carry out a series of arithmetic operations, assigning results to variables, to find the roots of a quadratic equation $ax^2 + bx + c = 0$. The conditional IF-THEN or IF-THEN-ELSE control structure allows a program to follow alternative paths of execution. Iteration, or looping, gives computers much of their power. They can repeat a sequence of steps as often as necessary and appropriate repetitions of quite simple steps can solve complex problems.

These control structures can be combined. A sequence may contain several loops; a loop may contain a loop nested within it, or the two branches of a conditional may each contain sequences with loops and more conditionals. In the "pseudocode", "*" indicates multiplication and "←" is used to assign values to variables. The following programming fragment employs the IF-THEN structure for finding one root of the quadratic equation, using the quadratic formula:

The quadratic formula assumes that a is nonzero and that the discriminant (the portion within the square root sign) is not negative (in order to obtain a real number root). Conditionals check those assumptions:

- IF $a = 0$ THEN
- ROOT ← $-c/b$
- ELSE
- DISCRIMINANT ← $b*b - 4*a*c$
- IF DISCRIMINANT ≥ 0 THEN
- ROOT ← $(-b + \text{SQUARE\_ROOT(DISCRIMINANT)})/2*a$
- ENDIF
- ENDIF

The SQUARE_ROOT function used in the above fragment is an example of a subprogram (also called a procedure, subroutine, or function). A subprogram is like a sauce recipe given once and used as part of many other recipes. Subprograms take inputs (the quantity needed) and produce results (the sauce). Commonly used subprograms are generally in a collection or library provided with a language. Subprograms may call other subprograms in their definitions, as shown by the following routine (where ABS is the absolute-value function). SQUARE_ROOT is implemented by using a WHILE (indefinite) loop that produces a good approximation for the square root of real numbers unless x is very small or very large. A subprogram is written by declaring its name, the type of input data, and the output:

- FUNCTION SQUARE_ROOT(REAL x) RETURNS REAL

- ROOT $\leftarrow$ 1.0

- WHILE ABS(ROOT*ROOT $- x$) $\geq$ 0.000001

- AND WHILE ROOT $\leftarrow$ (x/ROOT + ROOT)/2

- RETURN ROOT

Subprograms can break a problem into smaller, more tractable subproblems. Sometimes a problem may be solved by reducing it to a subproblem that is a smaller version of the original. In that case the routine is known as a recursive subprogram because it solves the problem by repeatedly calling itself. For example, the factorial functions in mathematics (n! = n·(n−1)············3·2·1—i.e., the product of the first n integers), can be programmed as a recursive routine:

- FUNCTION FACTORIAL(INTEGER n) RETURNS INTEGER

- IF n = 0 THEN RETURN 1

- ELSE RETURN n * FACTORIAL($n-1$)

The advantage of recursion is that it is often a simple restatement of a precise definition, one that avoids the bookkeeping details of an iterative solution.

At the machine-language level, loops and conditionals are implemented with branch instructions that say "jump to" a new point in the program. The "goto" statement in higher-level languages expresses the same operation but is rarely used because it makes it difficult for humans to follow the "flow" of a program. Some languages, such as Java and Ada, do not allow it.

Data Structures

Whereas control structures organize algorithms, data structures organize information. In particular, data structures specify types of data, and thus which operations can be performed on them, while eliminating the need for a programmer to keep track of memory addresses. Simple data structures include integers, real numbers, Booleans and characters or character strings. Compound data structures are formed by combining one or more data types.

The most important compound data structures are the array, a homogeneous collection of data, and the record, a heterogeneous collection. An array may represent a vector of numbers, a list of strings, or a collection of vectors (an array of arrays, or mathematical matrix). A record might store employee information—name, title, and salary. An array of records, such as a table of employees, is a collection of elements, each of which is heterogeneous. Conversely, a record might contain a vector—i.e., an array.

Record components, or fields, are selected by name; for example, E.SALARY might represent the salary field of record E. An array element is selected by its position or index; A[10] is the element at position 10 in array A. A FOR loop (definite iteration) can thus run through an array with index limits (FIRST TO LAST in the following example) in order to sum its elements:

- FOR $i \leftarrow$ FIRST TO LAST

- SUM $\leftarrow$ SUM $+ A[i]$

Arrays and records have fixed sizes. Structures that can grow are built with dynamic allocation, which provides new storage as required. These data structures have components, each containing data and references to further components (in machine terms, their addresses). Such self-referential structures have recursive definitions. A bintree (binary tree) for example, either is empty or contains a root component with data and left and right bintree "children." Such bintrees implement tables of information efficiently. Subroutines to operate on them are naturally recursive; the following routine prints out all the elements of a bintree (each is the root of some subtree):

- PROCEDURE TRAVERSE(ROOT: BINTREE)

- IF NOT(EMPTY(ROOT))

- TRAVERSE(ROOT.LEFT)

- PRINT ROOT.DATA

- TRAVERSE(ROOT.RIGHT)

- ENDIF

Abstract data types (ADTs) are important for large-scale programming. They package data structures and operations on them, hiding internal details. For example, an ADT table provides insertion and lookup operations to users while keeping the underlying structure, whether an array, list, or binary tree, invisible. In object-oriented languages, classes are ADTs and objects are instances of them. The following object-oriented pseudocode example assumes that there is an ADT bintree and a "superclass" COMPARABLE, characterizing data for which there is a comparison operation (such as "<" for integers). It defines a new ADT, TABLE that hides its data-representation and provides operations appropriate to tables. This class is polymorphic—defined in terms of an element-type parameter of the COMPARABLE class. Any instance of it must specify that type, here a class with employee data (the COMPARABLE declaration means that PERS_REC must provide a comparison operation to sort records). Implementation details are omitted.

- CLASS TABLE OF <COMPARABLE T>

- PRIVATE DATA: BINTREE OF <T>

- PUBLIC INSERT(ITEM: T)

- PUBLIC LOOKUP(ITEM: T) RETURNS BOOLEAN

- END

- CLASS PERS_REC: COMPARABLE

- PRIVATE NAME: STRING

- PRIVATE POSITION: {STAFF, SUPERVISOR, MANAGER}

- PRIVATE SALARY: REAL

- PUBLIC COMPARE (R: PERS_REC) RETURNS BOOLEAN

- END

- EMPLOYEES: TABLE <PERS_REC>

TABLE makes public only its own operations; thus, if it is modified to use an array or list rather than a bintree, programs that use it cannot detect the change. This information hiding is essential to managing complexity in large programs. It divides them into small parts, with "contracts" between the parts; here the TABLE class contracts to provide lookup and insertion operations, and its users contract to use only the operations so publicized.

Components of Programming Language

There are a number of important components in a programming language. A few of them are variables, arrays, functions, characters, loops and syntax diagrams. This chapter has been carefully written to provide an easy understanding of the varied facets of these components of programming languages.

Variables

Variables are the names you give to computer memory locations which are used to store values in a computer program.

For example, assume you want to store two values 10 and 20 in your program and at a later stage, you want to use these two values. Here are the following three simple steps:

- Create variables with appropriate names.

- Store your values in those two variables.

- Retrieve and use the stored values from the variables.

Creating Variables

Creating variables is also called declaring variables in C programming. Different programming languages have different ways of creating variables inside a program.

For example, C programming has the following simple way of creating variables–

```
#include <stdio.h>


int main() {
    int a;
    int b;
}
```

The above program creates two variables to reserve two memory locations with names a and b. We created these variables using int keyword to specify variable data type which means we want to store integer values in these two variables. Similarly, you can create variables to store long, float, char or any other data type.

For example:

```
/* variable to store long value */

long a;
```

```
/* variable to store float value */

float b;
```

You can create variables of similar type by putting them in a single line but separated by comma as follows –

```
#include <stdio.h>


int main() {

    int a, b;

}
```

Listed below are the key points about variables that you need to keep in mind –

- A variable name can hold a single type of value. For example, if variable a has been defined int type, then it can store only integer.

- C programming language requires a variable creation, i.e., declaration before its usage in your program. You cannot use a variable name in your program without creating it, though programming language like Python allows you to use a variable name without creating it.

- You can use a variable name only once inside your program. For example, if a variable a has been defined to store an integer value, then you cannot define a again to store any other type of value.

- There are programming languages like Python, PHP, Perl, etc., which do not want you to specify data type at the time of creating variables. So you can store integer, float, or long without specifying their data type.

- You can give any name to a variable like age, sex, salary, year1990 or anything else you like to give, but most of the programming languages allow to use only limited characters in their variables names. For now, we will suggest to use only a....z, A....Z, 0....9 in your variable names and start their names using alphabets only instead of digits.

- Almost none of the programming languages allow to start their variable names with a digit, so 1990year will not be a valid variable name whereas year1990 or ye1990ar are valid variable names.

Every programming language provides more rules related to variables and you will learn them when you will go in further detail of that programming language.

Store Values in Variables

Now, let's store some values in those variables –

```
#include <stdio.h>


int main() {
    int a;
    int b;


    a = 10;
    b = 20;
}
```

The above program has two additional statements where we are storing 10 in variable a and 20 is being stored in variable b. Almost all the programming languages have similar way of storing values in variable where we keep variable name in the left hand side of an equal sign = and whatever value we want to store in the variable, we keep that value in the right hand side.

Now, we have completed two steps, first we created two variables and then we stored required values in those variables. Now variable a has value 10 and variable b has value 20. In other words we can say, when above program is executed, the memory location named a will hold 10 and memory location b will hold 20.

Access Stored Values in Variables

If we do not use the stored values in the variables, then there is no point in creating variables and storing values in them. We know that the above program has two variables a and b and they store the values 10 and 20, respectively. So let's try to print the values stored in these two variables. Following is a C program, which prints the values stored in its variables.

```
#include <stdio.h>

int main() {
    int a;
    int b;

    a = 10;
    b = 20;

    printf( "Value of a = %d\n", a );
    printf( "Value of b = %d\n", b );
}
```

When the above program is executed, it produces the following result–

```
Value of a = 10

Value of b = 20
```

we are using printf() function to print the values of variables. We are making use of %d, which will be replaced with the values of the given variable in printf() statements. We can print both the values using a single printf() statement as follows –

```
#include <stdio.h>

int main() {
    int a;
    int b;

    a = 10;
    b = 20;

    printf( "Value of a = %d and value of b = %d\n", a, b );
}
```

When the above program is executed, it produces the following result–

```
Value of a = 10 and value of b = 20
```

If you want to use float variable in C programming, then you will have to use %f instead of %d, and if you want to print a character value, then you will have to use %c. Similarly, different data types can be printed using different % and characters.

Variables in Java

Following is the equivalent program written in Java programming language. This program will create two variables a and b and very similar to C programming, it will assign 10 and 20 in these variables and finally print the values of the two variables in two ways–

```
public class DemoJava {

    public static void main(String []args) {

        int a;

        int b;


        a = 10;

        b = 20;


        System.out.println("Value of a = " + a);

        System.out.println("Value of b = " + b);

        System.out.println("Value of a = " + a + " and value of b = " + b);

    }

}
```

When the above program is executed, it produces the following result–

```
Value of a = 10
Value of b = 20
Value of a = 10 and value of b = 20
```

Variables in Python

Following is the equivalent program written in Python. This program will create two variables a and b and at the same time, assign 10 and 20 in those variables.

Python does not want you to specify the data type at the time of variable creation and there is no need to create variables in advance.

```
a = 10

b = 20

print "Value of a = ", a

print "Value of b = ", b

print "Value of a = ", a, " and value of b = ", b
```

When the above program is executed, it produces the following result–

```
Value of a = 10

Value of b = 20

Value of a = 10   and value of b =   20
```

You can use the following syntax in C and Java programming to declare variables and assign values at the same time–

```
#include <stdio.h>


int main () {

    int a = 10;

    int b = 20;


    printf( "Value of a = %d and value of b = %d\n", a, b );

}
```

When the above program is executed, it produces the following result–

```
Value of a = 10 and value of b = 20
```

Arrays

An array can be defined as an ordered collection of items indexed by contiguous integers. Consider a situation where we need to store five integer numbers. If we use programming's simple variable and data type concepts, then we need five variables of int data type and the program will be as follows –

```
#include <stdio.h>
```

```
int main() {

    int number1;

    int number2;

    int number3;

    int number4;

    int number5;


    number1 = 10;

    number2 = 20;

    number3 = 30;

    number4 = 40;

    number5 = 50;


    printf( "number1: %d\n", number1);

    printf( "number2: %d\n", number2);

    printf( "number3: %d\n", number3);

    printf( "number4: %d\n", number4);

    printf( "number5: %d\n", number5);

}
```

It was simple, because we had to store just five integer numbers. Now let's assume we have to store 5000 integer numbers. Are we going to use 5000 variables?

To handle such situations, almost all the programming languages provide a concept called array. An array is a data structure, which can store a fixed-size collection of elements of the same data type. An array is used to store a collection of data, but it is often more useful to think of an array as a collection of variables of the same type.

Instead of declaring individual variables, such as number1, number2, ..., number99, you just declare one array variable number of integer type and use number1[0], number1[1], and ..., number1[99] to represent individual variables. Here, 0, 1, 2, ...99 are index associated with var variable and they are being used to represent individual elements available in the array.

All arrays consist of contiguous memory locations. The lowest address corresponds to the first element and the highest address to the last element.

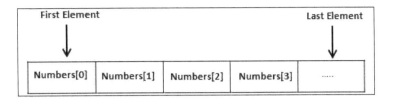

Create Arrays

To create an array variable in C, a programmer specifies the type of the elements and the number of elements to be stored in that array. Given below is a simple syntax to create an array in C programming:

```
type arrayName [ arraySize ];
```

This is called a single-dimensional array. The arraySize must be an integer constant greater than zero and type can be any valid C data type. For example, now to declare a 10-element array called number of type int, use this statement:

```
int number[10];
```

Here, number is a variable array, which is sufficient to hold up to 10 integer numbers.

Initializing Arrays

You can initialize an array in C either one by one or using a single statement as follows –

```
int number[5] = {10, 20, 30, 40, 50};
```

The number of values between braces { } cannot be larger than the number of elements that we declare for the array between square brackets [ ].

If you omit the size of the array, an array just big enough to hold the initialization is created. Therefore, if you write:

```
int number[] = {10, 20, 30, 40, 50};
```

You will create exactly the same array as you did in the previous example. Following is an example to assign a single element of the array:

```
number[4] = 50;
```

The above statement assigns element number 5th in the array with a value of 50. All arrays have 0 as the index of their first element which is also called the base index and the last index of an array will be the total size of the array minus 1. The following image shows the pictorial representation of the array.

Index	0	1	2	3	4
number	10	20	30	40	50

Accessing Array Elements

An element is accessed by indexing the array name. This is done by placing the index of the element within square brackets after the name of the array. For example:

```
int var = number[9];
```

The above statement will take the 10th element from the array and assign the value to var variable.

```
#include <stdio.h>


int main () {

    int number[10]; /* number is an array of 10 integers */

    int i = 0;


    /* Initialize elements of array n to 0 */

    while ( i < 10 ) {


        /* Set element at location i to i + 100 */

        number[ i ] = i + 100;

        i = i + 1;

    }


    /* Output each array element's value */

    i = 0;

    while ( i < 10 ) {


        printf("number[%d] = %d\n", i, number[i] );

        i = i + 1;

    }


    return 0;

}
```

When the above code is compiled and executed, it produces the following result:

```
number[0] = 100

number[1] = 101

number[2] = 102

number[3] = 103

number[4] = 104

number[5] = 105

number[6] = 106

number[7] = 107

number[8] = 108

number[9] = 109
```

Arrays in Java

Following is the equivalent program written in Java. Java supports arrays, but there is a little difference in the way they are created in Java using the new operator.

You can try to execute the following program to see the output, which must be identical to the result generated by the above C example.

```
public class DemoJava {

    public static void main(String []args) {

        int[] number = new int[10];

        int i = 0;


        while( i < 10 ) {


            number[ i ] = i + 100;

            i = i + 1;

        }


        i = 0;

        while( i < 10 ) {

            System.out.format( "number[%d] = %d\n", i, number[i] );
```

```
        i = i + 1;

    }

  }

}
```

When the above program is executed, it produces the following result:

```
number[0] = 100

number[1] = 101

number[2] = 102

number[3] = 103

number[4] = 104

number[5] = 105

number[6] = 106

number[7] = 107

number[8] = 108

number[9] = 109
```

Arrays in Python

Python does not have a concept of Array, instead Python provides another data structure called list, which provides similar functionality as arrays in any other language.

Following is the equivalent program written in Python:

```
# Following defines an empty list.

number = []

i = 0


while i < 10:

    # Appending elements in the list

    number.append(i + 100)

    i = i + 1


i = 0
```

```
while i < 10:

    # Accessing elements from the list

    print "number[", i,  "] = ", number[ i ]

    i = i + 1
```

When the above program is executed, it produces the following result:

```
number[ 0 ] =   100

number[ 1 ] =   101

number[ 2 ] =   102

number[ 3 ] =   103

number[ 4 ] =   104

number[ 5 ] =   105

number[ 6 ] =   106

number[ 7 ] =   107

number[ 8 ] =   108

number[ 9 ] =   109
```

Function

A function is a block of organized, reusable code that is used to perform a single, related action. Functions provide better modularity for your application and a high degree of code reusing.

Functions "Encapsulate" a task (they combine many instructions into a single line of code). Most programming languages provide many built in functions that would otherwise require many steps to accomplish, for example computing the square root of a number.

When a function is "called" the program "leaves" the current section of code and begins to execute the first line inside the function. Thus the function "flow of control" is:

1. The program comes to a line of code containing a "function call".

2. The program enters the function (starts at the first line in the function code).

3. All instructions inside of the function are executed from top to bottom.

4. The program leaves the function and goes back to where it started from.

5. Any data computed and RETURNED by the function is used in place of the function in the original line of code.

Need for Writing Functions

1. They allow us to conceive of our program as a bunch of sub-steps. (Each sub-step can be its own function. When any program seems too hard, just break the overall program into sub-steps).

2. They allow us to reuse code instead of rewriting it.

3. Functions allow us to keep our variable namespace clean (local variables only "live" as long as the function does). In other words, function_1 can use a variable called i, and function_2 can also use a variable called i and there is no confusion. Each variable i only exists when the computer is executing the given function.

4. Functions allow us to test small parts of our program in isolation from the rest. This is especially true in interpreted langaues, such as Matlab, but can be useful in C, Java, ActionScript, etc.

Steps to Writing a Function

1. Understand the purpose of the function.

2. Define the data that comes into the function from the caller (in the form of parameters).

3. Define what data variables are needed inside the function to accomplish its goal.

4. Decide on the set of steps that the program will use to accomplish this goal.

Parts of a Function

Functions can be called "black boxes" because we don't need to know how they work. Just what is supposed to go into them, and what is supposed to come out of them.

When defining a program as a black box, we must describe the following attributes of the function:

1. The Name - describes the purpose of the function. Usually a verb or phrase, such as "compute_Average", or just "average".

2. The Inputs - called parameters. Describe what data is necessary for the function to work and gives each piece of data a Symbolic Name for use in the function.

3. The Calculation - varies for each function.

4. The Output - Usually one (but sometimes zero or sometimes many) values that are calculated inside the function and "returned" via the output variables.

Function Workspace

Every function has its own workspace. This means that every variable inside the function is only usable during the execution of the function (and then the variables go away).

Having a separate "workspace" for each function is critical to proper software engineering. If every function shared every variable in an entire program, it would be easy to inadvertently change the values of variables that you shouldn't. Further, it would be hard to remember what "names" have been used elsewhere, and coming up with new names to represent similar ideas would be challenging.

A side-effect of function variables not existing after the end of the function is that the only way to get information "out" of a function is by "returning" that information via the output of the function.

Additionally, the function can only "see" the information that is "passed" to it via parameters. Thus the only way information can get "in" to the function is by using parameters.

Note: In certain object oriented languages (e.g., C++, Java, ActionScript), a function can also see all of the variables associated with its containing object.

Formal vs. Actual Parameters

When we create a function, it should represent a "generic" action that can be applied in many circumstances. For example, if we want to find the average grade, it doesn't matter if it is on a test, or on a quiz, or an assignment, or a midterm, etc. given any list of grades we can compute an average but if it can be any list of grades, how do we know what the list of grades will be called? The answer: we don't care. You, the programmer of the function, provide your own name for the data. This is much the same as when a sales person calls you and reads a script trying to sell something to you, they say: Dear _insert customer name here_, let me sell you our wonderful product.

When writing a function, the programmer must provide a blank to plug in what ever data is of current interest; the blank should have a good symbolic name saying what it will represent. Here is a pseudocode function example:

```
function average_grade( list_of_grades )

....end function
```

Inside the average_grade function, the name list_of_grades will be used in place of whatever variable some other user has stored his or her grades in. Thus to call the function, I might write:

```
// This some other code (not the function code)

        midterm_grades = ... // create array of grades

print "the average of the midterm was"

print average_grade( midterm_grades )
```

In this code, the grades are stored in the variable, "midterm_grades". Inside the function, the grades are stored in the variable "list_of_grades". Thus, during the execution of the program, both names will refer to the same thing but at different times.

The parameter "list_of_grades" is called a Formal paramater; again, this just means a place holder name for any possible set of grades.

The variable midterm_grades is the Actual paramater. This means "what is actually used" for this call to the function, such as [90, 100, 70].

Characters

Characters are simple alphabets like a, b, c, d...., A, B, C, D,......, but with an exception. In computer programming, any single digit number like 0, 1, 2,....and special characters like $, %, +, -.... etc., are also treated as characters and to assign them in a character type variable, you simply need to put them inside single quotes. For example, the following statement defines a character type variable ch and we assign a value 'a' to it:

```
char ch = 'a';
```

Here, ch is a variable of character type which can hold a character of the implementation's character set and 'a' is called a character literal or a character constant. Not only a, b, c,.... but when any number like 1, 2, 3.... or any special character like !, @, #, #, $,.... is kept inside single quotes, then they will be treated as a character literal and can be assigned to a variable of character type, so the following is a valid statement:

```
char ch = '1';
```

A character data type consumes 8 bits of memory which means you can store anything in a character whose ASCII value lies in between -127 to 127, so it can hold any of the 256 different values. A character data type can store any of the characters available on your keyboard including special characters like, @, #, #, $, %, ^, &, *, (,), _, +, {, }, etc.

Note that you can keep only a single alphabet or a single digit number inside single quotes and more than one alphabet or digits are not allowed inside single quotes. So the following statements are invalid in C programming:

```
char ch1 = 'ab';
```

```
char ch2 = '10';
```

Given below is a simple example, which shows how to define, assign, and print characters in C Programming language:

```
#include <stdio.h>


int main() {
    char   ch1;
    char   ch2;
    char   ch3;
    char   ch4;


    ch1 = 'a';
    ch2 = '1';
```

```
ch3 = '$';

ch4 = '+';


printf ( "ch1: %c\n", ch1);

printf ( "ch2: %c\n", ch2);

printf ( "ch3: %c\n", ch3);

printf ( "ch4: %c\n", ch4);
}
```

Here, we used %c to print a character data type. When the above program is executed, it produces the following result:

```
ch1: a

ch2: 1

ch3: $

ch4: +
```

Escape Sequences

Many programming languages support a concept called Escape Sequence. When a character is preceded by a backslash (\), it is called an escape sequence and it has a special meaning to the compiler. For example, \n in the following statement is a valid character and it is called a new line character –

```
char ch = '\n';
```

Here, character n has been preceded by a backslash (\), it has special meaning which is a new line but keep in mind that backslash (\) has special meaning with a few characters only. The following statement will not convey any meaning in C programming and it will be assumed as an invalid statement –

```
char ch = '\1';
```

The following table lists the escape sequences available in C programming language –

Escape Sequence	Description
\t	Inserts a tab in the text at this point.
\b	Inserts a backspace in the text at this point.
\n	Inserts a new line in the text at this point.
\r	Inserts a carriage return in the text at this point.
\f	Inserts a form feed in the text at this point.
\'	Inserts a single quote character in the text at this point.
\"	Inserts a double quote character in the text at this point.
\\	Inserts a backslash character in the text at this point.

The following example shows how the compiler interprets an escape sequence in a print statement:

```
#include <stdio.h>


int main() {
    char   ch1;
    char   ch2;
    char   ch3;
    char   ch4;


    ch1 = '\t';
    ch2 = '\n';


    printf( "Test for tabspace %c and a newline %c will start here", ch1, ch2);
}
```

When the above program is executed, it produces the following result–

Test for tabspace and a newline will start here.

Characters in Java

Following is the equivalent program written in Java. Java handles character data types much in the same way as we have seen in C programming. However, Java provides additional support for character manipulation.

You can try to execute the following program to see the output, which must be identical to the result generated by the above C example.

```
public class DemoJava {
    public static void main(String []args) {
        char   ch1;
        char   ch2;
        char   ch3;
        char   ch4;


        ch1 = 'a';
```

```
        ch2  =  '1';

        ch3  =  '$';

        ch4  =  '+';


        System.out.format( "ch1: %c\n", ch1);

        System.out.format( "ch2: %c\n", ch2);

        System.out.format( "ch3: %c\n", ch3);

        System.out.format( "ch4: %c\n", ch4);

    }

}
```

When the above program is executed, it produces the following result –

```
ch1:    a

ch2:    1

ch3:    $

ch4:    +
```

Java also supports escape sequence in the same way you have used them in C programming.

Characters in Python

Python does not support any character data type but all the characters are treated as string, which is a sequence of characters. You do not need to have any special arrangement while using a single character in Python.

Following is the equivalent program written in Python –

```
ch1  =  'a';

ch2  =  '1';

ch3  =  '$';

ch4  =  '+';


print "ch1: ", ch1
```

```
print "ch2: ", ch2

print "ch3: ", ch3

print "ch4: ", ch4
```

When the above program is executed, it produces the following result:

```
ch1:    a

ch2:    1

ch3:    $

ch4:    +
```

Loops

Let's consider a situation when you want to print Hello, World! five times. Here is a simple C program to do the same.

```
#include <stdio.h>


int main() {

    printf( "Hello, World!\n");

    printf( "Hello, World!\n");

    printf( "Hello, World!\n");

    printf( "Hello, World!\n");

    printf( "Hello, World!\n");

}
```

When the above program is executed, it produces the following result:

```
Hello, World!

Hello, World!

Hello, World!

Hello, World!

Hello, World!
```

It was simple, but again, let's consider another situation when you want to write Hello, World! a thousand times. We can certainly not write printf () statements a thousand times. Almost all the programming languages provide a concept called loop, which helps in executing one or more statements up to a desired number of times. All high-level programming languages provide various forms of loops, which can be used to execute one or more statements repeatedly.

Let's write the above C program with the help of a while loop.

```
#include <stdio.h>


int main() {
    int i = 0;


    while ( i < 5 ) {
        printf( "Hello, World!\n");
        i = i + 1;

    }

}
```

When the above program is executed, it produces the following result –

```
Hello, World!

Hello, World!

Hello, World!

Hello, World!

Hello, World!
```

The above program makes use of a while loop, which is being used to execute a set of programming statements enclosed within {....}. Here, the computer first checks whether the given condition, i.e., variable "a" is less than 5 or not and if it finds the condition is true, then the loop body is entered to execute the given statements. Here, we have the following two statements in the loop body:

- First statement is printf() function, which prints Hello World!

- Second statement is i = i + 1, which is used to increase the value of variable i.

After executing all the statements given in the loop body, the computer goes back to while (i < 5) and the given condition, (i < 5), is checked again, and the loop is executed again if the condition holds true. This process repeats till the given condition remains true which means variable "a" has a value less than 5.

To conclude, a loop statement allows us to execute a statement or group of statements multiple times. Given further is the general form of a loop statement in most of the programming languages.

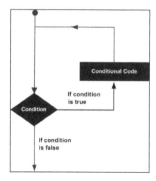

The While Loop

A while loop available in C Programming language has the following syntax:

```
while ( condition ) {

   /*....while loop body ....*/

}
```

The above code can be represented in the form of a flow diagram as shown below.

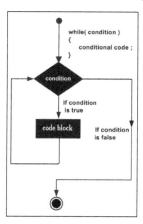

The following important points are to be noted about a while loop:

- A while loop starts with a keyword while followed by a condition enclosed in ( ).

- Further to the while() statement, you will have the body of the loop enclosed in curly braces {...}.

- A while loop body can have one or more lines of source code to be executed repeatedly.

- If the body of a while loop has just one line, then its optional to use curly braces {...}.

- A while loop keeps executing its body till a given condition holds true. As soon as the condition becomes false, the while loop comes out and continues executing from the immediate next statement after the while loop body.

- A condition is usually a relational statement, which is evaluated to either true or false. A value equal to zero is treated as false and any non-zero value works like true.

The do-while Loop

A while loop checks a given condition before it executes any statements given in the body part. C programming provides another form of loop, called do-while that allows to execute a loop body before checking a given condition. It has the following syntax:

```
do {

    /*....do...while loop body ....*/

}

while ( condition );
```

The above code can be represented in the form of a flow diagram as shown below.

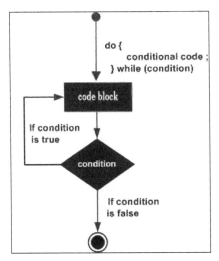

If you will write the above example using do-while loop, then Hello, World! will produce the same result:

```
#include <stdio.h>


int main() {

    int i = 0;


    do {

        printf( "Hello, World!\n");

        i = i + 1;

    }

    while ( i < 5 );

}
```

When the above program is executed, it produces the following result:

```
Hello, World!

Hello, World!

Hello, World!

Hello, World!

Hello, World!
```

The Break Statement

When the break statement is encountered inside a loop, the loop is immediately terminated and the program control resumes at the next statement following the loop. The syntax for a break statement in C is as follows:

```
break;
```

A break statement can be represented in the form of a flow diagram as shown below.

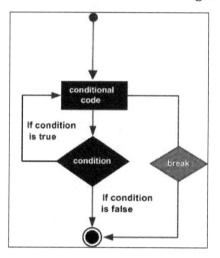

Following is a variant of the above program, but it will come out after printing Hello World! only three times:

```
#include <stdio.h>

int main() {

    int i = 0;

    do {

        printf( "Hello, World!\n");

        i = i + 1;


        if( i == 3 ) {
```

```
        break;

    }

  }

  while ( i < 5 );

}
```

When the above program is executed, it produces the following result:

```
Hello, World!

Hello, World!

Hello, World!
```

The Continue Statement

The continue statement in C programming language works somewhat like the break statement. Instead of forcing termination, continue forces the next iteration of the loop to take place, skipping any code in between. The syntax for a continue statement in C is as follows:

```
continue;
```

A continue statement can be represented in the form of a flow diagram as shown below.

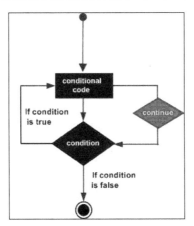

Following is a variant of the above program, but it will skip printing when the variable has a value equal to 3:

```
#include <stdio.h>

int main() {

    int i = 0;

    do {

        if( i == 3 ) {

            i = i + 1;
```

```
        continue;
    }
    printf( "Hello, World!\n");
    i = i + 1;
}
while ( i < 5 );
}
```

When the above program is executed, it produces the following result:

```
Hello, World!
Hello, World!
Hello, World!
Hello, World!
```

Loops in Java

Following is the equivalent program written in Java that too supports while and do while loops. The following program prints Hello, World! five times as we did in the case of C Programming.

You can try to execute the following program to see the output, which must be identical to the result generated by the above example.

```
public class DemoJava {
    public static void main(String []args) {
        int i = 0;

        while ( i < 5 ) {
            System.out.println("Hello, World!");
            i = i + 1;
        }
    }
}
```

The break and continue statements in Java programming work quite the same way as they work in C programming.

Loops in Python

Following is the equivalent program written in Python. Python too supports while and do while loops. The following program prints Hello, World! five times as we did in case of C Programming. Here you must note that Python does not make use of curly braces for the loop body, instead it simply identifies the body of the loop using indentation of the statements.

You can try to execute the following program to see the output. To show the difference, we have used one more print statement, which will be executed when the loop will be over.

```
i = 0


while (i < 5):

    print "Hello, World!"

    i = i + 1
print "Loop ends"
```

When the above program is executed, it produces the following result:

```
Hello, World!

Hello, World!

Hello, World!

Hello, World!

Hello, World!

Loop ends
```

The break and continue statements in Python work quite the same way as they do in C programming.

Syntax Diagram

Syntax diagrams are made up of a few specific symbols that together define any grammatical rule.

Symbol: A Circle with Some Text Inside

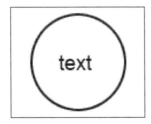

This is an item that is not defined in any more detail. There are no lower level syntax diagrams defining this any further. This is called a 'terminal symbol'.

This is because the item described is self-evident. For example if the number '1' was inside the circle, then there is no need to define what '1' means (unless you are a mathematician).

Symbol: A Rectangle with Some Text Inside

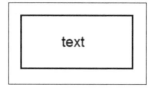

This is an item that is defined in some more greater detail in another syntax diagram. For example the text might be 'postal address' and because it is a rectangle rather than a circle, you should expect to see a syntax diagram describing the internal structure of 'postal-address'.

Symbol: Arrow

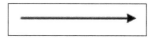

An arrow in a syntax diagram indicates the direction in which you are allowed to read the overall diagram. For example:

This shows you should read it from left to right.

An arrow that loops back to an earlier point indicates a repetition of the items in-between. For example:

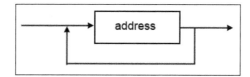

This indicates that there is at least one address, but there may be any number of additional addresses as well because the arrow is allowing you to read the item again and again.

References

- Computer-programming-variables, computer-programming: tutorialspoint.com, Retrieved 2 February, 2019
- Computer-programming-arrays, computer-programming: tutorialspoint.com, Retrieved 12 May, 2019
- Computer-programming-characters, computer-programming: tutorialspoint.com, Retrieved 14 January, 2019
- Computer-programming-loops, computer-programming: tutorialspoint.com, Retrieved 4 March, 2019

C++ Programming Language

C++ is the name of a general purpose programming language which is an extension of the C programming language. The topics elaborated in this chapter will help in gaining a better perspective about C++ as well as the different variables, functions, arrays and pointers in it.

C++ is an enhanced C language typically used for object oriented programming. It traces its origins back well over thirty years. Although it's far from the oldest computer language, it's one of the older ones that is in common usage today– so you might say it gets an A for its ability to adapt to changing technological times.

C++ was developed by Bjarne Stroustrup, who the first development worked as part of his PhD project. During the early years, he called the language "C with Classes". He had begun developing a new language because he felt that no existing language was ideal for large scale projects. Later, when he was working at AT&T Bell Labs, he again felt limited. He dusted off his "C with Classes" and added features of other languages. Simula had a strong influence; AlLGOL 68 played a role. Ultimately, a lot more than classes got added: virtual functions, templates, and operator overloading.

C++ has grown far beyond a one man operation. The name actually came from another developer, Rick Mascitti. It was partly a play on the name of the "++" operator and partly a reference to the enhancement; two pluses may have been a bit of a joke.

The language was first standardized in 1998. Standards were again issued in 2003, 2007, and 2011. C++ is maintained by the ISO, a large standards committee. The current version is C++11. According to Stroustrup, the biggest improvement is in abstraction mechanisms. Among the other goals of the most recent revision: to make C++ a better language for embedded systems and to better support novices.

Development has been guided by certain ideals. C++ strives to be portable; there is an attempt to avoid reliance on features that are platform-dependent.

The standard, of course, isn't all there is; there are libraries that exist outside it.

Use of C++

C++ is widely used in embedded systems software engineering. It's also popular in communications and gaming. It is used in many other industries: health care, finances, and even defense.

Facebook has posted ads that cite C++ among the desired skills. Other recent postings for those versed in C++ come from Verizon Wireless, WSFS Bank, and Lord & Taylor.

One reason that programmers opt for C++ is that it interfaces well with other languages. Another plus is that it is high performance.

The process of mining existing languages to create new ones has of course been ongoing. C++has influenced later languages like PHP, Java, and (not surprisingly) C# (C-Sharp).

Variables in C++

A variable is a name given to a memory location. It is the basic unit of storage in a program.

- The value stored in a variable can be changed during program execution.

- A variable is only a name given to a memory location, all the operations done on the variable effects that memory location.

- In C++, all the variables must be declared before use.

Declaring Variables

A typical variable declaration is of the form:

```
// Declaring a single variable

type variable_name;


// Declaring multiple variables:

type variable1_name, variable2_name, variable3_name;
```

A variable name can consist of alphabets (both upper and lower case), numbers and the underscore '_' character. However, the name must not start with a number.

In the above diagram:

- Datatype: Type of data that can be stored in this variable.

- Variable_name: Name given to the variable.

- Value: It is the initial value stored in the variable.

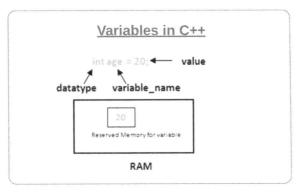

Variable in C++

Examples:

```
// Declaring float variable

float simpleInterest;


// Declaring integer variable

int time, speed;


// Declaring character variable

char var;
```

Difference between Variable Declaration and Definition

The variable declaration refers to the part where a variable is first declared or introduced before its first use. A variable definition is a part where the variable is assigned a memory location and a value. Most of the times, variable declaration and definition are done together.

See the following C++ program for better clarification:

```
#include <iostream>

using namespace std;


int main()

{

    // declaration and definition

    // of variable <a123>

    char a123 = 'a';
```

```
// This is also both declaration and definition
// as <b> is allocated memory and
// assigned some garbage value.
float b;

// multiple declarations and definitions
int _c, _d45, e;

// Let us print a variable
cout << a123 << endl;

return 0;
}
```

Output:

a

Types of Variables

There are three types of variables based on the scope of variables in C++:

- Local Variables
- Instance Variables
- Static Variables.

Let us now learn about each one of these variables in detail.

Local Variables

A variable defined within a block or method or constructor is called local variable.

- These variable are created when the block in entered or the function is called and destroyed after exiting from the block or when the call returns from the function.

- The scope of these variables exists only within the block in which the variable is declared. i.e. we can access these variable only within that block.

- Initilisation of local variable is mandatory.

Sample Programs

1. Sample Program

```cpp
// C++ program to demonstrate Local variables

#include <iostream>
using namespace std;

void StudentAge()
{
    // local variable age
    int age = 0;
    age = age + 5;
    cout << "Student age is : " << age;
}

// Driver code
int main()
{
    StudentAge();
}
```

Output:

```
Student age is : 5
```

In the above program, the variable age is a local variable to the function StudentAge(). If we use the variable age outside StudentAge() function, the compiler will produce an error as shown in below program.

Sample Program

2. Sample Program

```cpp
// C++ program to demonstrate Local variables
```

```
#include <iostream>

using namespace std;


void StudentAge()

{

    // local variable age

    int age = 0;

    age = age + 5;

}


// Driver code

int main()

{

    StudentAge();

    cout << "Student age is : " << age;

}
```

Instance Variables

Instance variables are non-static variables and are declared in a class outside any method, constructor or block.

- As instance variables are declared in a class, these variables are created when an object of the class is created and destroyed when the object is destroyed.

- Unlike local variables, we may use access specifiers for instance variables. If we do not specify any access specifier then the default access specifier will be used.

- Initilisation of instance variable is not mandatory.

- Instance variable can be accessed only by creating objects.

Sample Program

```
// C++ program to demonstrate Local variables


#include <iostream>

using namespace std;
```

```cpp
class Marks {

public:
    // This is a class variable
    static int studentNumber;


    // These variables are instance variables.
    // These variables are in a class
    // and are not inside any function
    int engMarks;
    int mathsMarks;
    int phyMarks;

public:
    Marks()
    {

        // Modify the class variable
        ++studentNumber;
    };
};

// Setting the class variable of Marks
int Marks::studentNumber = 0;


// Driver code
int main()
{
```

```
    // first object
    Marks obj1;
    obj1.engMarks = 50;
    obj1.mathsMarks = 80;
    obj1.phyMarks = 90;

    // second object
    Marks obj2;
    obj2.engMarks = 80;
    obj2.mathsMarks = 60;
    obj2.phyMarks = 85;

    // displaying marks for first object
    cout << "Marks for first object:\n";
    cout << Marks::studentNumber << endl;
    cout << obj1.engMarks << endl;
    cout << obj1.mathsMarks << endl;
    cout << obj1.phyMarks << endl;

    // displaying marks for second object
    cout << "Marks for second object:\n";
    cout << Marks::studentNumber << endl;
    cout << obj2.engMarks << endl;
    cout << obj2.mathsMarks << endl;
    cout << obj2.phyMarks << endl;
}
```

Output:

```
Marks for first object:
2
50
80
90
```

```
Marks for second object:

2

80

60

85
```

As you can see in the above program the variables, engMarks, mathsMarks, phyMarksare instance variables. In case we have multiple objects as in the above program, each object will have its own copies of instance variables. It is clear from the above output that each object will have its own copy of instance variable.

Static Variables

Static variables are also known as Class variables.

- These variables are declared similarly as instance variables, the difference is that static variables are declared using the static keyword within a class outside any method constructor or block.

- Unlike instance variables, we can only have one copy of a static variable per class irrespective of how many objects we create.

- Static variables are created at the start of program execution and destroyed automatically when execution ends.

- Initialization of Static Variable is not Mandatory. Its default value is 0.

- If we access the static variable like Instance variable (through an object), the compiler will show the warning message and it won't halt the program. The compiler will replace the object name to class name automatically.

- If we access the static variable without the class name, Compiler will automatically append the class name.

To access static variables, we need not create an object of that class, we can simply access the variable as:

```
class_name::variable_name;
```

Sample Program

```
// C++ program to demonstrate Static variables


#include <iostream>

using namespace std;
```

```cpp
class Marks {

public:

    // This is a class variable
    static int studentNumber;


    // These variables are instance variables.
    // These variables are in a class
    // and are not inside any function
    int engMarks;
    int mathsMarks;
    int phyMarks;


    Marks()
    {

        // Modify the class variable
        ++studentNumber;
    };
};


// Setting the class variable of Marks
int Marks::studentNumber = 0;


// Driver code
int main()
{

    // object of Marks
    Marks obj1;
    obj1.engMarks = 50;
```

```
obj1.mathsMarks = 80;

obj1.phyMarks = 90;


// displaying marks for first object

cout << "Marks for object:\n";


// Now to display the static variable,

// it can be directly done

// using the class name

cout << Marks::studentNumber << endl;


// But same is not the case

// with instance variables

cout << obj1.engMarks << endl;

cout << obj1.mathsMarks << endl;

cout << obj1.phyMarks << endl;
}
```

Output:

```
Marks for object:

1

50

80

90
```

Instance Variable vs. Static Variable

- Each object will have its own copy of instance variable whereas we can only have one copy of a static variable per class irrespective of how many objects we create.

- Changes made in an instance variable using one object will not be reflected in other objects as each object has its own copy of instance variable. In case of static, changes will be reflected in other objects as static variables are common to all object of a class.

- We can access instance variables through object references and static variables can be accessed directly using class name.

Syntax for static and instance variables:

```
class Example

{

    static int a; // static variable

    int b;        // instance variable

}
```

Scope of Variables in C++

In general, scope is defined as the extent upto which something can be worked with. In programming also scope of a variable is defined as the extent of the program code within which the variable can we accessed or declared or worked with. There are mainly two types of variable scopes as discussed below:

Local Variables

Variables defined within a function or block are said to be local to those functions.

- Anything between '{' and '}' is said to inside a block.

- Local variables do not exist outside the block in which they are declared, i.e. they can not be accessed or used outside that block.

- Declaring local variables: Local variables are declared inside a block.

```
// CPP program to illustrate

// usage of local variables

#include<iostream>

using namespace std;


void func()

{

    // this variable is local to the

    // function func() and cannot be

    // accessed outside this function

    int age=18;

}


int main()
```

```
{
    cout<<"Age is: "<<age;

    return 0;
}
```

Output:

```
Error: age was not declared in this scope
```

The above program displays an error saying "age was not declared in this scope". The variable age was declared within the function func() so it is local to that function and not visible to portion of program outside this function.

Rectified Program: To correct the above error we have to display the value of variable age from the function func() only. This is shown in the below program:

```
// CPP program to illustrate
// usage of local variables
#include<iostream>
using namespace std;

void func()
{
    // this variable is local to the
    // function func() and cannot be
    // accessed outside this function
    int age=18;
    cout<<age;
}

int main()
{
    cout<<"Age is: ";
    func();

    return 0;
}
```

Output:

```
Age is: 18
```

Global Variables

As the name suggests, global variables can be accessed from any part of the program.

- They are available through out the life time of a program.

- They are declared at the top of the program outside all of the functions or blocks.

- Declaring global variables: Global variables are usually declared outside of all of the functions and blocks, at the top of the program. They can be accessed from any portion of the program.

```cpp
// CPP program to illustrate
// usage of global variables
#include<iostream>
using namespace std;


// global variable
int global = 5;


// global variable accessed from
// within a function
void display()
{
    cout<<global<<endl;
}


// main function
int main()
{
    display();

    // changing value of global
    // variable from main function
```

```
    global = 10;

    display();
}
```

Output:

5

10

In the program, the variable "global" is declared at the top of the program outside all of the functions so it is a global variable and can be accessed or updated from anywhere in the program.

```
#include<iostream>
using namespace std;   Global Variable

// global variable
int global = 5;

// main function
int main()                              Local variable
{
    // local variable with same
    // name as that of global variable
    int global = 2;

    cout << global << endl;
}
```

If there is a variable inside a function with the same name as that of a global variable and if the function tries to access the variable with that name, then which variable will be given precedence? Local variable or Global variable? Look at the below program to understand the question:

```
// CPP program to illustrate

// scope of local variables

// and global variables together

#include<iostream>

using namespace std;


// global variable

int global = 5;


// main function

int main()
```

```
{
    // local variable with same
    // name as that of global variable

    int global = 2;
    cout << global << endl;
}
```

Look at the above program. The variable "global" declared at the top is global and stores the value 5 where as that declared within main function is local and stores a value 2. So, the question is when the value stored in the variable named "global" is printed from the main function then what will be the output? 2 or 5?

- Usually when two variable with same name are defined then the compiler produces a compile time error. But if the variables are defined in different scopes then the compiler allows it.

- Whenever there is a local variable defined with same name as that of a global variable then the compiler will give precedence to the local variable.

Here in the above program also, the local variable named "global" is given precedence. So the output is 2.

Accessing a global variable when there is a local variable with same name.

What if we want to do the opposite of above task. What if we want to access global variable when there is a local variable with same name?

To solve this problem we will need to use the scope resolution operator. Below program explains how to do this with the help of scope resolution operator.

```
// C++ program to show that we can access a global
// variable using scope resolution operator :: when
// there is a local variable with same name
#include<iostream>
using namespace std;

// Global x
int x = 0;
```

```
int main()
{
  // Local x
  int x = 10;
  cout << "Value of global x is " << ::x;
  cout<< "\nValue of local x is " << x;
  return 0;
}
```

Output:

```
Value of global x is 0
Value of local x is 10
```

Flow Control in C++

If Else Statement in C++

Sometimes we need to execute a block of statements only when a particular condition is met or not met. This is called decision making, as we are executing a certain code after making a decision in the program logic. For decision making in C++, we have four types of control statements (or control structures), which are as follows:

- If statement
- Nested if statement
- If-else statement
- If-else-if statement.

If Statement in C++

If statement consists a condition, followed by statement or a set of statements as shown below:

```
if(condition){
  Statement(s);
}
```

The statements inside if parenthesis (usually referred as if body) gets executed only when the given condition is true. If the condition is false then the statements inside if body are completely ignored.

Flow Diagram of if Statement

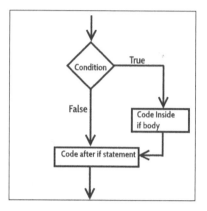

Example of if statement:

```cpp
#include <iostream>
using namespace std;
int main(){
   int num=70;
   if( num < 100 ){
      /* This cout statement will only execute,
       * if the above condition is true
       */
      cout<<"number is less than 100";
   }


   if(num > 100){
      /* This cout statement will only execute,
       * if the above condition is true
       */
      cout<<"number is greater than 100";
   }
   return 0;
}
```

Output:

```
number is less than 100
```

Nested if Statement in C++

When there is an if statement inside another if statement then it is called the nested if statement.

The structure of nested if looks like this:

```
if(condition_1) {
    Statement1(s);

    if(condition_2) {
        Statement2(s);
    }
}
```

Statement1 would execute if the condition_1 is true. Statement2 would only execute if both the conditions (condition_1 and condition_2) are true.

Example of Nested if statement:

```cpp
#include <iostream>
using namespace std;
int main(){
    int num=90;
    /* Nested if statement. An if statement
     * inside another if body
     */
    if( num < 100 ){
        cout<<"number is less than 100"<<endl;
        if(num > 50){
            cout<<"number is greater than 50";
        }
    }
    return 0;
}
```

Output:

```
number is less than 100
number is greater than 50
```

if-else Statement in C++

Sometimes you have a condition and you want to execute a block of code if condition is true and execute another piece of code if the same condition is false. This can be achieved in C++ using if-else statement.

This is how an if-else statement looks:

```
if(condition) {

    Statement(s);

}

else {

    Statement(s);

}
```

The statements inside "if" would execute if the condition is true, and the statements inside "else" would execute if the condition is false.

Flow Diagram of if-else

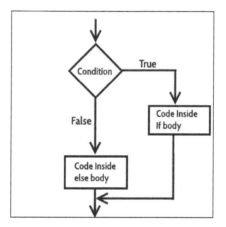

Example of if-else statement:

```
#include <iostream>

using namespace std;

int main(){

    int num=66;

    if( num < 50 ){

        //This would run if above condition is true

        cout<<"num is less than 50";

    }
```

```
   else {

      //This would run if above condition is false

      cout<<"num is greater than or equal 50";

   }

   return 0;

}
```

Output:

```
num is greater than or equal 50
```

if-else-if Statement in C++

if-else-if statement is used when we need to check multiple conditions. In this control structure we have only one "if" and one "else", however we can have multiple "else if" blocks. This is how it looks:

```
if(condition_1) {

   /*if condition_1 is true execute this*/

   statement(s);

}
else if(condition_2) {

   /* execute this if condition_1 is not met and

    * condition_2 is met

    */

   statement(s);

}
else if(condition_3) {

   /* execute this if condition_1 & condition_2 are

    * not met and condition_3 is met

    */

   statement(s);

}
 .

 .

 .else {
```

```
/* if none of the condition is true
 * then these statements gets executed
 */
statement(s);
}
```

The most important point to note here is that in if-else-if, as soon as the condition is met, the corresponding set of statements get executed, rest gets ignored. If none of the condition is met then the statements inside "else" gets executed.

Example of if-else-if:

```
#include <iostream>
using namespace std;
int main(){
    int num;
    cout<<"Enter an integer number between 1 & 99999: ";
    cin>>num;
    if(num <100 && num>=1) {
        cout<<"Its a two digit number";
    }
    else if(num <1000 && num>=100) {
        cout<<"Its a three digit number";
    }
    else if(num <10000 && num>=1000) {
        cout<<"Its a four digit number";
    }
    else if(num <100000 && num>=10000) {
        cout<<"Its a five digit number";
    }
    else {
        cout<<"number is not between 1 & 99999";
    }
    return 0;
}
```

Output:

```
Enter an integer number between 1 & 99999: 8976
Its a four digit number
```

C++ Switch Case

Switch case statement is used when we have multiple conditions and we need to perform different action based on the condition. When we have multiple conditions and we need to execute a block of statements when a particular condition is satisfied. In such case either we can use lengthy if-else-if statement or switch case. The problem with lengthy if-else-if is that it becomes complex when we have several conditions. The switch case is a clean and efficient method of handling such scenarios.

The syntax of Switch case statement:

```
switch (variable or an integer expression)
{
    case constant:
    //C++ code
    ;
    case constant:
    //C++ code
    ;
    default:
    //C++ code
    ;
}
```

Switch Case statement is mostly used with break statement even though the break statement is optional.

Example of Switch Case:

```
#include <iostream>
using namespace std;
int main(){
    int num=5;
    switch(num+2) {
        case 1:
            cout<<"Case1: Value is: "<<num<<endl;
```

```
    case 2:

      cout<<"Case2: Value is: "<<num<<endl;

    case 3:

      cout<<"Case3: Value is: "<<num<<endl;

    default:

      cout<<"Default: Value is: "<<num<<endl;

  }

    return 0;

}
```

Output:

```
Default: Value is: 5
```

Explanation: In switch I gave an expression, you can give variable as well. I gave the expression num+2, where num value is 5 and after addition the expression resulted 7. Since there is no case defined with value 4 the default case got executed.

Switch Case Flow Diagram

It evaluates the value of expression or variable (based on whatever is given inside switch braces), then based on the outcome it executes the corresponding case.

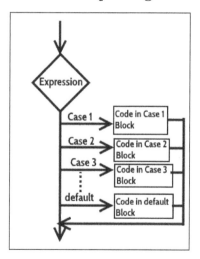

Break Statement in Switch Case

Before we discuss about break statement, Let's see what happens when we don't use break statement in switch case. See the example below:

```
#include <iostream>

using namespace std;
```

```
int main(){
    int i=2;
    switch(i) {
        case 1: cout<<"Case1 "<<endl;
        case 2: cout<<"Case2 "<<endl;
        case 3: cout<<"Case3 "<<endl;
        case 4: cout<<"Case4 "<<endl;
        default: cout<<"Default "<<endl;
    }
    return 0;
}
```

Output:

```
Case2
Case3
Case4
Default
```

In the above program, we have the variable i inside switch braces, which means whatever the value of variable i is, the corresponding case block gets executed. We have passed integer value 2 to the switch, so the control switched to the case 2, however we don't have break statement after the case 2 that caused the flow to continue to the subsequent cases till the end. However this is not what we wanted, we wanted to execute the right case block and ignore rest blocks. The solution to this issue is to use the break statement in after every case block.

Break statements are used when you want your program-flow to come out of the switch body. Whenever a break statement is encountered in the switch body, the execution flow would directly come out of the switch, ignoring rest of the cases. This is why you must end each case block with the break statement.

Let's take the same example but this time with break statement.

```
#include <iostream>
using namespace std;
int main(){
    int i=2;
    switch(i) {
        case 1:
```

```
        cout<<"Case1 "<<endl;

        break;
    case 2:

        cout<<"Case2 "<<endl;

        break;
    case 3:

        cout<<"Case3 "<<endl;

        break;
    case 4:

        cout<<"Case4 "<<endl;

        break;
    default:

        cout<<"Default "<<endl;

    }

    return 0;

}
```

Output:

```
Case2
```

Now you can see that only case 2 got executed, rest of the subsequent cases were ignored.

Why didn't we use break statement after default?

The control would itself come out of the switch after default so we didn't use break statement after it, however if you want you can use it, there is no harm in doing that.

- Case doesn't always need to have order 1, 2, 3 and so on. It can have any integer value after case keyword. Also, case doesn't need to be in an ascending order always, you can specify them in any order based on the requirement.

- You can also use characters in switch case. For example:

```
#include <iostream>

using namespace std;

int main(){

    char ch='b';

    switch(ch) {
```

```
    case 'd': cout<<"Case1 ";

    break;

    case 'b': cout<<"Case2 ";

    break;

    case 'x': cout<<"Case3 ";

    break;

    case 'y': cout<<"Case4 ";

    break;

    default: cout<<"Default ";

  }

  return 0;

}
```

- Nesting of switch statements are allowed, which means you can have switch statements inside another switch. However nested switch statements should be avoided as it makes program more complex and less readable.

For Loop in C++

A loop is used for executing a block of statements repeatedly until a particular condition is satisfied. For example, when you are displaying number from 1 to 100 you may want set the value of a variable to 1 and display it 100 times, increasing its value by 1 on each loop iteration.

In C++ we have three types of basic loops: for, while and do-while.

Syntax of for Loop

```
for(initialization; condition ; increment/decrement)

{

   C++ statement(s);

}
```

Flow of Execution of the for Loop

As a program executes, the interpreter always keeps track of which statement is about to be executed. We call this the control flow, or the flow of execution of the program.

- First step: In for loop, initialization happens first and only once, which means that the initialization part of for loop only executes once.

- Second step: Condition in for loop is evaluated on each loop iteration, if the condition is true then the statements inside for for loop body gets executed. Once the condition returns false, the statements in for loop does not execute and the control gets transferred to the next statement in the program after for loop.

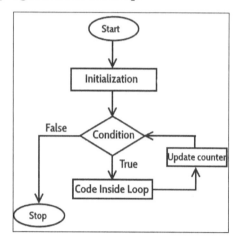

- Third step: After every execution of for loop's body, the increment/decrement part of for loop executes that updates the loop counter.

- Fourth step: After third step, the control jumps to second step and condition is re-evaluated.

The steps from second to fourth repeats until the loop condition returns false.

Example of a Simple for Loop in C++

Here in the loop initialization part, the value of variable i to 1, condition is i<=6 and on each loop iteration the value of i increments by 1 has been set.

```cpp
#include <iostream>

using namespace std;

int main(){

    for(int i=1; i<=6; i++){

        /* This statement would be executed

        * repeatedly until the condition

        * i<=6 returns false.

        */

        cout<<"Value of variable i is: "<<i<<endl;

    }

    return 0;

}
```

```
Value of variable i is: 1

Value of variable i is: 2

Value of variable i is: 3

Value of variable i is: 4

Value of variable i is: 5

Value of variable i is: 6
```

Infinite for Loop in C++

A loop is said to be infinite when it executes repeatedly and never stops. This usually happens by mistake. When you set the condition in for loop in such a way that it never return false, it becomes infinite loop.

For example:

```cpp
#include <iostream>

using namespace std;

int main(){

    for(int i=1; i>=1; i++){

        cout<<"Value of variable i is: "<<i<<endl;

    }

    return 0;

}
```

This is an infinite loop as we are incrementing the value of i so it would always satisfy the condition i>=1, the condition would never return false.

Here is another example of infinite for loop:

```cpp
// infinite loop

for ( ; ; ) {

    // statement(s)

}
```

Example: Display elements of array using for loop.

```cpp
#include <iostream>

using namespace std;

int main(){
```

```
int arr[]={21,9,56,99, 202};
/* We have set the value of variable i
 * to 0 as the array index starts with 0
 * which means the first element of array
 * starts with zero index.
 */
for(int i=0; i<5; i++){
    cout<<arr[i]<<endl;
}
return 0;
}
```

Output:

```
21
9
56
99
202
```

C++ While Loop

Syntax of While Loop

```
while(condition)
{
    statement(s);
}
```

Working Principle of While Loop

In while loop, condition is evaluated first and if it returns true then the statements inside while loop execute, this happens repeatedly until the condition returns false. When condition returns false, the control comes out of loop and jumps to the next statement in the program after while loop.

The important point to note when using while loop is that we need to use increment or decrement statement inside while loop so that the loop variable gets changed on each iteration, and at some point condition returns false. This way we can end the execution of while loop otherwise the loop would execute indefinitely.

Flow Diagram of While Loop

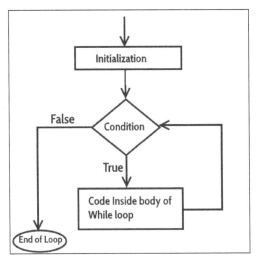

While Loop example in C++:

```cpp
#include <iostream>
using namespace std;
int main(){
    int i=1;
    /* The loop would continue to print
     * the value of I until the given condition
     * i<=6 returns false.
     */
    while(i<=6){
        cout<<"Value of variable I is: "<<i<<endl; i++;
    }
}
```

Output:

```
Value of variable I is: 1
Value of variable I is: 2
Value of variable I is: 3
Value of variable I is: 4
Value of variable I is: 5
Value of variable I is: 6
```

Infinite While Loop

A while loop that never stops is said to be the infinite while loop, when we give the condition in such a way so that it never returns false, then the loops becomes infinite and repeats itself indefinitely.

An example of infinite while loop:

This loop would never end as we're decrementing the value of I which is 1 so the condition i<=6 would never return false.

```
#include <iostream>
using namespace std;
int main(){
    int i=1; while(i<=6) {
        cout<<"Value of variable I is: "<<i<<endl; i--;
    }
}
```

Example: Displaying the elements of array using while loop.

```
#include <iostream>
using namespace std;
int main(){
    int arr[]={21,87,15,99, -12};
    /* The array index starts with 0, the
     * first element of array has 0 index
     * and represented as arr[0]
     */
    int i=0;
    while(i<5){
        cout<<arr[i]<<endl;
        i++;
    }
}
```

Output:

```
21
87
15
99
-12
```

C++ do-while Loop

Syntax of do-while Loop

```
do
{
    statement(s);
} while(condition);
```

Working Principle of do-while Loop

First, the statements inside loop execute and then the condition gets evaluated, if the condition returns true then the control jumps to the "do" for further repeated execution of it, this happens repeatedly until the condition returns false. Once condition returns false control jumps to the next statement in the program after do-while.

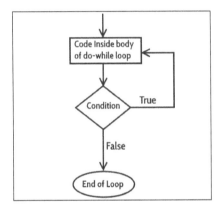

Do-while loop example in C++:

```
#include <iostream>
using namespace std;
int main() {
    int num=1;
    do{
        cout<<"Value of num: "<<num<<endl;
        num++;
    }while(num<=6);
    return 0;
}
```

Output:

```
Value of num: 1
```

Value of num: 2

Value of num: 3

Value of num: 4

Value of num: 5

Value of num: 6

Example: Displaying array elements using do-while loop.

Here we have an integer array which has four elements. We are displaying the elements of it using do-while loop.

```cpp
#include <iostream>
using namespace std;
int main(){
    int arr[]={21,99,15,109};
    /* Array index starts with 0, which
     * means the first element of array
     * is at index 0, arr[0]
     */
    int i=0;
    do{
        cout<<arr[i]<<endl;
        i++;
    }while(i<4);
    return 0;
}
```

Output:

21

99

15

109

Continue Statement in C++

Continue statement is used inside loops. Whenever a continue statement is encountered inside a loop, control directly jumps to the beginning of the loop for next iteration, skipping the execution of statements inside loop's body for the current iteration.

Syntax of Continue Statement

```
continue;
```

Example: Continue statement inside for loop.

As you can see that the output is missing the value 3, however the for loop iterate though the num value 0 to 6. This is because we have set a condition inside loop in such a way, that the continue statement is encountered when the num value is equal to 3. So for this iteration the loop skipped the cout statement and started the next iteration of loop.

```cpp
#include <iostream>

using namespace std;

int main(){

    for (int num=0; num<=6; num++) {

        /* This means that when the value of

         * num is equal to 3 this continue statement

         * would be encountered, which would make the

         * control to jump to the beginning of loop for

         * next iteration, skipping the current iteration

         */


        if (num==3) {

            continue;

        }

        cout<<num<<" ";

    }

    return 0;

}
```

Output:

```
0 1 2 4 5 6
```

Flow Diagram of Continue Statement

Example: Use of continue in While loop.

```cpp
#include <iostream>
using namespace std;
int main(){
    int j=6;
    while (j >=0) {
        if (j==4) {
            j--;
            continue;
        }
        cout<<"Value of j: "<<j<<endl;
        j--;
    }
    return 0;
}
```

Output:

```
Value of j: 6
Value of j: 5
Value of j: 3
Value of j: 2
Value of j: 1
Value of j: 0
```

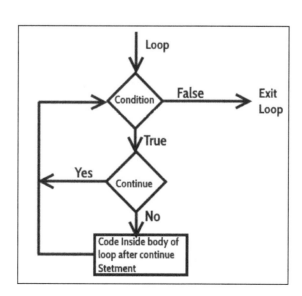

Example of continue in do-While loop:

```cpp
#include <iostream>
using namespace std;
int main(){
    int j=4;
    do {
        if (j==7) {
            j++;
            continue;
        }
        cout<<"j is: "<<j<<endl;
        j++;
    }while(j<10);
    return 0;
}
```

Output:

```
j is: 4
j is: 5
j is: 6
j is: 8
j is: 9
```

Break Statement in C++

The break statement is used in following two scenarios:

a) Use break statement to come out of the loop instantly. Whenever a break statement is encountered inside a loop, the control directly comes out of loop terminating it. It is used along with if statement, whenever used inside loop so that it occurs only for a particular condition.

b) It is used in switch case control structure after the case blocks. Generally all cases in switch case are followed by a break statement to avoid the subsequent cases execution. Whenever it is encountered in switch-case block, the control comes out of the switch-case body.

Syntax of Break Statement

```cpp
break;
```

Break Statement Flow Diagram

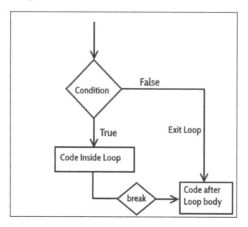

Example – Use of break statement in a while loop:

In the example below, we have a while loop running from 10 to 200 but since we have a break statement that gets encountered when the loop counter variable value reaches 12, the loop gets terminated and the control jumps to the next statement in program after the loop body.

```cpp
#include <iostream>
using namespace std;
int main(){
    int num =10;
    while(num<=200) {
        cout<<"Value of num is: "<<num<<endl;
        if (num==12) {
            break;
        }
        num++;
    }
    cout<<"Hey, I'm out of the loop";
    return 0;
}
```

Output:

```
Value of num is: 10
Value of num is: 11
Value of num is: 12
Hey, I'm out of the loop
```

Example: Break statement in for loop.

```
#include <iostream>
using namespace std;
int main(){
    int var;
    for (var =200; var>=10; var --) {
        cout<<"var: "<<var<<endl;
        if (var==197) {
            break;
        }
    }
    cout<<"Hey, I'm out of the loop";
    return 0;
}
```

Output:

```
var: 200
var: 199
var: 198
var: 197
Hey, I'm out of the loop
```

Example: Break statement in Switch Case.

```
#include <iostream>
using namespace std;
int main(){
    int num=2;
    switch (num) {
        case 1: cout<<"Case 1 "<<endl;
        break;
        case 2: cout<<"Case 2 "<<endl;
        break;
```

```
    case 3: cout<<"Case 3 "<<endl;

    break;

    default: cout<<"Default "<<endl;

  }

  cout<<"Hey, I'm out of the switch case";

  return 0;

}
```

Output:

```
Case 2

Hey, I'm out of the switch case
```

In this example, we have break statement after each case block, this is because if we don't have it then the subsequent case block would also execute. The output of the same program without break would be:

```
Case 2

Case 3

Default

Hey, I'm out of the switch case
```

Goto Statement in C++

The Goto statement is used for transferring the control of a program to a given label. The syntax of goto statement looks like this:

```
goto label_name;
```

Program Structure

```
label1:

...

...

goto label2;

...

..

label2:

...
```

In a program we have any number of goto and label statements, the goto statement is followed by a label name, whenever goto statement is encountered, the control of the program jumps to the label specified in the goto statement.

Goto statements are almost never used in any development as they are complex and makes your program much less readable and more error prone. In place of goto, you can use continue and break statement.

Example of goto statement in C++:

```cpp
#include <iostream>

using namespace std;

int main(){

    int num; cout<<"Enter a number: "; cin>>num;

    if (num % 2==0){

        goto print;

    }

    else {

        cout<<"Odd Number";

    }

    print:

    cout<<"Even Number";

    return 0;

}
```

Output:

```
Enter a number: 42
Even Number
```

Functions in C++

A function is a group of statements that together perform a task. Every C++ program has at least one function, which is main, and all the most trivial programs can define additional functions.

You can divide up your code into separate functions. How you divide up your code among different functions is up to you, but logically the division usually is such that each function performs a specific task.

A function declaration tells the compiler about a function's name, return type, and parameters. A function definition provides the actual body of the function.

The C++ standard library provides numerous built-in functions that your program can call. For example, function strcat() to concatenate two strings, function memcpy() to copy one memory location to another location and many more functions.

A function is known with various names like a method or a sub-routine or a procedure etc.

Defining a Function

The general form of a C++ function definition is as follows:

```
return_type function_name( parameter list ) {

   body of the function

}
```

A C++ function definition consists of a function header and a function body. Here are all the parts of a function:

- Return type: A function may return a value. The return_type is the data type of the value the function returns. Some functions perform the desired operations without returning a value. In this case, the return_type is the keyword void.

- Function name: This is the actual name of the function. The function name and the parameter list together constitute the function signature.

- Parameters: A parameter is like a placeholder. When a function is invoked, you pass a value to the parameter. This value is referred to as actual parameter or argument. The parameter list refers to the type, order, and number of the parameters of a function. Parameters are optional; that is, a function may contain no parameters.

- Function body – The function body contains a collection of statements that define what the function does.

Example:

Following is the source code for a function called max(). This function takes two parameters num1 and num2 and return the biggest of both:

```
// function returning the max between two numbers


int max(int num1, int num2) {
   // local variable declaration
   int result;


   if (num1 > num2)
      result = num1;
```

```
   else

      result = num2;


   return result;

}
```

Function Declarations

A function declaration tells the compiler about a function name and how to call the function. The actual body of the function can be defined separately.

A function declaration has the following parts:

```
return_type function_name ( parameter list );
```

For the above defined function max(), following is the function declaration:

```
int max(int num1, int num2);
```

Parameter names are not important in function declaration only their type is required, so following is also valid declaration:

```
int max(int, int);
```

Function declaration is required when you define a function in one source file and you call that function in another file. In such case, you should declare the function at the top of the file calling the function.

Calling a Function

While creating a C++ function, you give a definition of what the function has to do. To use a function, you will have to call or invoke that function.

When a program calls a function, program control is transferred to the called function. A called function performs defined task and when it's return statement is executed or when its function-ending closing brace is reached, it returns program control back to the main program.

To call a function, you simply need to pass the required parameters along with function name, and if function returns a value, then you can store returned value. For example:

```
#include <iostream>
using namespace std;


// function declaration
int max(int num1, int num2);
```

```
int main () {

    // local variable declaration:

    int a = 100;

    int b = 200;

    int ret;


    // calling a function to get max value.

    ret = max(a, b);

    cout << "Max value is : " << ret << endl;


    return 0;

}


// function returning the max between two numbers

int max(int num1, int num2) {

    // local variable declaration

    int result;


    if (num1 > num2)

        result = num1;

    else

        result = num2;


    return result;

}
```

Kept max() function along with main() function and compiled the source code. While running final executable, it would produce the following result:

```
Max value is: 200
```

Function Arguments

If a function is to use arguments, it must declare variables that accept the values of the arguments. These variables are called the formal parameters of the function.

The formal parameters behave like other local variables inside the function and are created upon entry into the function and destroyed upon exit.

While calling a function, there are two ways that arguments can be passed to a function.

Sr. No	Call Type & Description
1	Call by Value: This method copies the actual value of an argument into the formal parameter of the function. In this case, changes made to the parameter inside the function have no effect on the argument.
2	Call by Pointer: This method copies the address of an argument into the formal parameter. Inside the function, the address is used to access the actual argument used in the call. This means that changes made to the parameter affect the argument.
3	Call by Reference: This method copies the reference of an argument into the formal parameter. Inside the function, the reference is used to access the actual argument used in the call. This means that changes made to the parameter affect the argument.

By default, C++ uses call by value to pass arguments. In general, this means that code within a function cannot alter the arguments used to call the function and above mentioned example while calling max() function used the same method.

Default Values for Parameters

When you define a function, you can specify a default value for each of the last parameters. This value will be used if the corresponding argument is left blank when calling to the function.

This is done by using the assignment operator and assigning values for the arguments in the function definition. If a value for that parameter is not passed when the function is called, the default given value is used, but if a value is specified, this default value is ignored and the passed value is used instead. Consider the following example –

```cpp
#include <iostream>

using namespace std;


int sum(int a, int b = 20) {

    int result;

    result = a + b;


    return (result);

}

int main () {
```

```
// local variable declaration:

int a = 100;

int b = 200;

int result;


// calling a function to add the values.

result = sum(a, b);

cout << "Total value is :" << result << endl;


// calling a function again as follows.

result = sum(a);

cout << "Total value is :" << result << endl;


    return 0;

}
```

When the above code is compiled and executed, it produces the following result –

```
Total value is:300

Total value is:120
```

Arrays in C++

An array is a collection of similar items stored in contiguous memory locations. In programming, sometimes a simple variable is not enough to hold all the data. For example, lets say we want to store the marks of 500 students, having 500 different variables for this task is not feasible, we can define an array with size 500 that can hold the marks of all students.

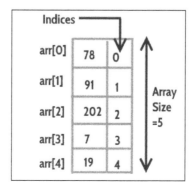

Declaring an array in C++

There are couple of ways to declare an array.

Method 1:

```
int arr[5];
arr[0] = 10;
arr[1] = 20;
arr[2] = 30;
arr[3] = 40;
arr[4] = 50;
```

Method 2:

```
int arr[] = {10, 20, 30, 40, 50};
```

Method 3:

```
int arr[5] = {10, 20, 30, 40, 50};
```

Accessing Array Elements

Array index starts with 0, which means the first array element is at index 0, second is at index 1 and so on. We can use this information to display the array elements. See the code below:

```
#include <iostream>
using namespace std;
int main(){
    int arr[] = {11, 22, 33, 44, 55};
    cout<<arr[0]<<endl;
    cout<<arr[1]<<endl;
    cout<<arr[2]<<endl;
    cout<<arr[3]<<endl;
    cout<<arr[4]<<endl;
    return 0;
}
```

Output:

```
11
22
```

33

44

55

Although this code worked fine, displaying all the elements of array like this is not recommended. When you want to access a particular array element then this is fine but if you want to display all the elements then you should use a loop like this:

```cpp
#include <iostream>
using namespace std;


int main(){
    int arr[] = {11, 22, 33, 44, 55};
    int n=0;


    while(n<=4){
        cout<<arr[n]<<endl;
        n++;
    }
    return 0;
}
```

Multidimensional Arrays in C++

Multidimensional arrays are also known as array of arrays. The data in multidimensional array is stored in a tabular form as shown in the diagram below:

	column 1	column 2	column 3	column 4	column 5
row1	arr[0][0]	arr[0][1]	arr[0][2]	arr[0][3]	arr[0][4]
row2	arr[1][0]	arr[1][1]	arr[1][2]	arr[1][3]	arr[1][4]
row3	arr[2][0]	arr[2][1]	arr[2][2]	arr[2][3]	arr[2][4]

A Two Dimensional Array

```cpp
int arr[2][3];
```

This array has total 2*3 = 6 elements.

A Three Dimensional Array

```
int arr[2][2][2];
```

This array has total 2*2*2 = 8 elements.

Two Dimensional Array

Lets see how to declare, initialize and access two dimensional array elements.

How to declare a two dimensional array?

```
int myarray[2][3];
```

Initialization

We can initialize the array in many ways:

Method 1:

```
int arr[2][3] = {10, 11 ,12 ,20 ,21 , 22};
```

Method 2:

This way of initializing is preferred as you can visualize the rows and columns here.

```
int arr[2][3] = {{10, 11 ,12} , {20 ,21 , 22}};
```

Accessing Array Elements

arr[0][0] – first element

arr[0][1] – second element

arr[0][2] – third element

arr[1][0] – fourth element

arr[1][1] – fifth element

arr[1][2] – sixth element

Example: Two dimensional array in C++.

```
#include <iostream>
using namespace std;
int main(){
   int arr[2][3] = {{11, 22, 33}, {44, 55, 66}};
   for(int i=0;  i<2;i++){
      for(int j=0; j<3; j++){
```

```
        cout<<"arr["<<i<<"]["<<j<<"]: "<<arr[i][j]<<endl;

    }

  }

    return 0;

}
```

Output:

```
arr[0][0]: 11

arr[0][1]: 22

arr[0][2]: 33

arr[1][0]: 44

arr[1][1]: 55

arr[1][2]: 66
```

Three Dimensional Array

Lets see how to declare, initialize and access Three Dimensional Array elements.

Declaring a Three Dimensional Array

```
int myarray[2][3][2];
```

Initialization

We can initialize the array in many ways:

Method 1:

```
int arr[2][3][2] = {1, -1 ,2 ,-2 , 3 , -3, 4, -4, 5, -5, 6, -6};
```

Method 2:

This way of initializing is preferred as you can visualize the rows and columns here.

```
int arr[2][3][2] = {
      { {1,-1}, {2, -2}, {3, -3}},
      { {4, -4}, {5, -5}, {6, -6}}
}
```

Three Dimensional Array Example

```
#include <iostream>
using namespace std;
```

```cpp
int main(){
    // initializing the array
    int arr[2][3][2] = {
        { {1,-1}, {2,-2}, {3,-3} },
        { {4,-4}, {5,-5}, {6,-6} }
    };
    // displaying array values
    for (int x = 0; x < 2; x++) {
        for (int y = 0; y < 3; y++) {
            for (int z = 0; z < 2; z++) {
                cout<<arr[x][y][z]<<" ";
            }
        }
    }
    return 0;
}
```

Output:

```
1 -1 2 -2 3 -3 4 -4 5 -5 6 -6
```

Passing Array to Function in C++

You can pass array as an argument to a function just like you pass variables as arguments. In order to pass array to the function you just need to mention the array name during function call like this:

```cpp
function_name(array_name);
```

Example: Passing arrays to a function.

In this example, we are passing two arrays a & b to the function sum(). This function adds the corresponding elements of both the arrays and display them.

```cpp
#include <iostream>
using namespace std;
/* This function adds the corresponding
 * elements of both the arrays and
 * displays it.
```

```
*/
void sum(int arr1[], int arr2[]){
    int temp[5];
    for(int i=0; i<5; i++){
        temp[i] = arr1[i]+arr2[i];
        cout<<temp[i]<<endl;
    }
}
int main(){
    int a[5] = {10, 20, 30, 40 ,50};
    int b[5] = {1, 2, 3, 4, 5};
    //Passing arrays to function
    sum(a, b);
    return 0;
}
```

Output:

11

22

33

44

55

Example: Passing multidimensional array to function.

In this example we are passing a multidimensional array to the function square which displays the square of each element.

```
#include <iostream>
#include <cmath>
using namespace std;
/* This method prints the square of each
 * of the elements of multidimensional array
 */
void square(int arr[2][3]){
```

```
   int temp;
   for(int i=0; i<2; i++){
      for(int j=0; j<3; j++){
         temp = arr[i][j];
         cout<<pow(temp, 2)<<endl;
      }
   }
}
int main(){
   int arr[2][3] = {
         {1, 2, 3},
         {4, 5, 6}
   };
   square(arr);
   return 0;
}
```

Output:

1

4

9

16

25

36

Strings in C++

Strings are words that are made up of characters, hence they are known as sequence of characters. In C++ we have two ways to create and use strings: 1) By creating char arrays and treat them as string 2) By creating string object.

Let's discuss these two ways of creating string first and then we will see which method is better and why.

Array of Characters – Also Known as C Strings

Example:

A simple example where we have initialized the char array during declaration.

```
#include <iostream>

using namespace std;

int main(){

    char book[50] = "A Song of Ice and Fire";

    cout<<book;

    return 0;

}
```

Output:

```
A Song of Ice and Fire
```

Example: Getting user input as string.

This can be considered as inefficient method of reading user input, why? Because when we read the user input string using cin then only the first word of the string is stored in char array and rest get ignored. The cin function considers the space in the string as delimiter and ignores the part after it.

```
#include <iostream>

using namespace std;

int main(){

    char book[50];

    cout<<"Enter your favorite book name:";

    //reading user input

    cin>>book;

    cout<<"You entered: "<<book;

    return 0;

}
```

Output:

```
Enter your favorite book name:The Murder of Roger Ackroyd
```

```
You entered: The
```

You can see that only the "The" got captured in the book and remaining part after space got ignored. How to deal with this then? Well, for this we can use cin.get function, which reads the complete line entered by user.

Example: Correct way of capturing user input string using cin.get.

```
#include <iostream>
```

```
using namespace std;
int main(){
    char book[50];
    cout<<"Enter your favorite book name:";


    //reading user input
    cin.get(book, 50);
    cout<<"You entered: "<<book;
    return 0;
}
```

Output:

```
Enter your favorite book name:The Murder of Roger Ackroyd
You entered: The Murder of Roger Ackroyd
```

Drawback of this Method

1) Size of the char array is fixed, which means the size of the string created through it is fixed in size, more memory cannot be allocated to it during runtime. For example, lets say you have created an array of character with the size 10 and user enters the string of size 15 then the last five characters would be truncated from the string.

On the other hand if you create a larger array to accommodate user input then the memory is wasted if the user input is small and array is much larger then what is needed.

2) In this method, you can only use the in-built functions created for array which don't help much in string manipulation.

Solution of these Problems

We can create string using string object. Let's see how we can do it.

String object in C++

Till now we have seen how to handle strings in C++ using char arrays. Let's see another and better way of handling strings in C++ – string objects.

```
#include<iostream>
using namespace std;
int main(){
    // This is how we create string object
```

```
    string str;
    cout<<"Enter a String:";
    /* This is used to get the user input
     * and store it into str
     */
    getline(cin,str);
    cout<<"You entered: ";
    cout<<str<<endl;
    /* This function adds a character at
     * the end of the string
     */ str.push_back('A');
    cout<<"The string after push_back: "<<str<<endl;
    /* This function deletes a character from
     * the end of the string
     */
    str.pop_back();
    cout << "The string after pop_back: "<<str<<endl;
    return 0;
}
```

Output:

```
Enter a String:XYZ
You entered: XYZ
The string after push_back: XYZA
The string after pop_back: XYZ
```

The advantage of using this method is that you need not to declare the size of the string, the size is determined at run time, so this is better memory management method. The memory is allocated dynamically at runtime so no memory is wasted.

Pointers in C++

The pointer in C++ language is a variable, it is also known as locator or indicator that points to an address of a value.

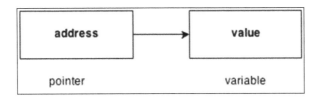

Advantages of Pointer

1. Pointer reduces the code and improves the performance, it is used to retrieving strings, trees etc. and used with arrays, structures and functions.

2. We can return multiple values from function using pointer.

3. It makes you able to access any memory location in the computer's memory.

Usage of Pointer

There are many usage of pointers in C++ language.

1. Dynamic memory allocation:

    In c language, we can dynamically allocate memory using malloc() and calloc() functions where pointer is used.

2. Arrays, Functions and Structures:

    Pointers in c language are widely used in arrays, functions and structures. It reduces the code and improves the performance.

Symbols used in Pointer

Symbol	Name	Description
& (ampersand sign)	Address operator	Determine the address of a variable.
* (asterisk sign)	Indirection operator	Access the value of an address.

Declaring a Pointer

The pointer in C++ language can be declared using * (asterisk symbol).

```
int * a; //pointer to int
char * c; //pointer to char
```

Pointer Example

Let's see the simple example of using pointers printing the address and value.

```
#include <iostream>
using namespace std;
```

```
int main()
{
int number=30;
int *   p;
p=&number;//stores the address of number variable
cout<<"Address of number variable is:"<<&number<<endl;
cout<<"Address of p variable is:"<<p<<endl;
cout<<"Value of p variable is:"<<*p<<endl;
    return 0;
}
```

Output:

```
Address of number variable is:0x7ffccc8724c4
Address of p variable is:0x7ffccc8724c4
Value of p variable is:30
```

Pointer program to swap 2 numbers without using 3rd variable.

```
#include <iostream>
using namespace std;
int main()
{
int a=20,b=10,*p1=&a,*p2=&b;
cout<<"Before swap: *p1="<<*p1<<" *p2="<<*p2<<endl;
*p1=*p1+*p2;
*p2=*p1-*p2;
*p1=*p1-*p2;
cout<<"After swap: *p1="<<*p1<<" *p2="<<*p2<<endl;
    return 0;
}
```

Output:

```
Before swap: *p1=20 *p2=10
After swap: *p1=10 *p2=20
```

References

- Cplusplus, programming-languages: softwareengineerinsider.com, Retrieved 18 April, 2019

- Variables-in-c: geeksforgeeks.org, Retrieved 8 January, 2019

- Scope-of-variables-in-c: geeksforgeeks.org, Retrieved 17 July, 2019

- Cpp-if-else-statement: beginnersbook.com, Retrieved 7 March, 2019

- Cpp-functions, cplusplus: tutorialspoint.com, Retrieved 19 August, 2019

- Cpp-arrays: beginnersbook.com, Retrieved 21 June, 2019

- Cpp-pointers: javatpoint.com, Retrieved 28 February, 2019

Hypertext Markup Language (HTML)

Hypertext Markup Language refers to the standard markup language which is used for documents that are designed to be displayed in a web browser. One of the most popular versions of hypertext markup language is HTML5. All the diverse principles of HTML5 as well as its applications have been carefully analyzed in this chapter.

HTML stands for Hypertext Markup Language. It allows the user to create and structure sections, paragraphs, headings, links, and blockquotes for web pages and applications.

HTML is not a programming language, meaning it doesn't have the ability to create dynamic functionality. Instead, it makes it possible to organize and format documents, similarly to Microsoft Word.

When working with HTML, we use simple code structures (tags and attributes) to mark up a website page. For example, we can create a paragraph by placing the enclosed text within a starting <p> and closing </p> tag.

<p>This is how you add a paragraph in HTML.</p>

<p>You can have more than one!</p>

Working Procedure of HTML

HTML documents are files that end with a .html or .htm extension. You can view then using any web browser (such as Google Chrome, Safari, or Mozilla Firefox). The browser reads the HTML file and renders its content so that internet users can view it.

Usually, the average website includes several different HTML pages. For instance: home pages, about pages, contact pages would all have separate HTML documents.

Each HTML page consists of a set of tags (also called elements), which you can refer to as the building blocks of web pages. They create a hierarchy that structures the content into sections, paragraphs, headings, and other content blocks.

Most HTML elements have an opening and a closing that use the <tag></tag> syntax.

Below, you can see a code example of how HTML elements can be structured:

```
<div>
```

<h1>The Main Heading</h1>

<h2>A catchy subheading</h2>

<p>Paragraph one</p>

```
<img src="/" alt="Image">
```

```
<p>Paragraph two with a <a href="https://example.com">hyperlink</a></p>
```

```
</div>
```

- The outmost element is a simple division (*<div></div>*) you can use to mark up bigger content sections.

- It contains a heading (*<h1></h1>*), a subheading (*<h2></h2>*), two paragraphs (*<p></p>*), and an image (*<img>*).

- The second paragraph includes a link (*<a></a>*) with a href attribute that contains the destination URL.

- The image tag also has two attributes: *src* for the image path and *alt* for the image description.

Overviewing the most used HTML Tags

HTML tags have two main types: block-level and inline tags.

- Block-level elements take up the full available space and always start a new line in the document. Headings and paragraphs are a great example of block tags.

- Inline elements only take up as much space as they need and don't start a new line on the page. They usually serve to format the inner contents of block-level elements. Links and emphasized strings are good examples of inline tags.

Block-Level Tags

The three block level tags every HTML document needs to contain are <html>, <head>, and <body>.

- The <html></html> tag is the highest level element that encloses every HTML page.

- The <head></head> tag holds meta information such as the page's title and charset.

- Finally, the <body></body> tag encloses all the content that appears on the page.

```
<html>
<head>
<!-- META INFORMATION -->
</head>
<body>
<!-- PAGE CONTENT -->
</body>
</html>
```

- Headings have 6 levels in HTML. They range from <h1></h1> to <h6></h6>, where h1 is the highest level heading and h6 is the lowest one. Paragraphs are enclosed by <p></p>, while blockquotes use the <blockquote></blockquote> tag.

- Divisions are bigger content sections that typically contain several paragraphs, images, sometimes blockquotes, and other smaller elements. We can mark them up using the <div></div> tag. A div element can contain another div tag inside it as well.

- You may also use <ol></ol> tags for ordered lists and <ul></ul> for unordered ones. Individual list items must be enclosed by the <li></li> tag. For example, this is how a basic unordered list looks like in HTML:

```
<ul>

<li>List item 1</li>

<li>List item 2</li>

<li>List item 3</li>

</ul>
```

Inline Tags

Many inline tags are used to format text. For example, a <strong></strong> tag would render an element in bold, whereas <em></em> tags would show it in italics.

Hyperlinks are also inline elements that require <a></a> tags and href attributes to indicate the link's destination:

```
<a href="https://example.com/">Click me!</a>
```

Images are inline elements too. You can add one using <img> without any closing tag. But you will also need to use the src attribute to specify the image path, for example:

```
<img src="/images/example.jpg" alt="Example image">
```

Pros and Cons of HTML

Like most things, HTML comes with a handful of strengths and limitations.

Pros

- A widely used language with a lot of resources and a huge community behind.

- Runs natively in every web browser.

- Comes with a flat learning curve.

- Open-source and completely free.

- Clean and consistent markup.

- The official web standards are maintained by the World Wide Web Consortium (W3C).

- Easily integrable with backend languages such as PHP and Node.js.

Cons

- Mostly used for static web pages. For dynamic functionality, you may need to use JavaScript or a backend language such as PHP.

- It does not allow the user to implement logic. As a result, all web pages need to be created separately, even if they use the same elements, e.g. headers and footers.

- Some browsers adopt new features slowly.

- Browser behavior is sometimes hard to predict (e.g. older browsers don't always render newer tags).

HTML Elements

An HTML element usually consists of a start tag and an end tag, with the content inserted in between:

`<tagname>`Content goes here `</tagname>`

The HTML element is everything from the start tag to the end tag:

`<p>`My first paragraph.`</p>`

Start tag	Element content	End tag
<h1>	My First Heading	</h1>
<p>	My first paragraph.	</p>

HTML elements with no content are called empty elements. Empty elements do not have an end tag, such as the <br> element (which indicates a line break).

Nested HTML Elements

HTML elements can be nested (elements can contain elements).

All HTML documents consist of nested HTML elements.

This example contains four HTML elements:

Example:

```
<!DOCTYPE html>

<html>

<body>

<h1>My First Heading</h1>

<p>My first paragraph.</p>

</body>

</html>
```

Explaination:

The <html> element defines the whole document.

It has a start tag <html> and an end tag </html>.

Inside the <html> element is the <body> element.

```
<html>
<body>
<h1>My First Heading</h1>
<p>My first paragraph.</p>
</body>
</html>
```

The <body> element defines the document body.

It has a start tag <body> and an end tag </body>.

Inside the <body> element is two other HTML elements: <h1> and <p>.

```
<body>
<h1>My First Heading</h1>
<p>My first paragraph.</p>
</body>
```

The <h1> element defines a heading.

It has a start tag <h1> and an end tag </h1>.

The element content is: My First Heading.

```
<h1>My First Heading</h1>
```

The <p> element defines a paragraph.

It has a start tag <p> and an end tag </p>.

The element content is: My first paragraph.

```
<p>My first paragraph.</p>
```

End Tag

Some HTML elements will display correctly, even if you forget the end tag:

Example:

```
<html>
```

```
<body>

<p>This is a paragraph

<p>This is a paragraph

</body>

</html>
```

The example above works in all browsers, because the closing tag is considered optional.

Never rely on this. It might produce unexpected results and/or errors if you forget the end tag.

Empty HTML Elements

HTML elements with no content are called empty elements.

 is an empty element without a closing tag (the <br> tag defines a line break):

Example:

```
<p>This is a <br> paragraph with a line break.</p>
```

Empty elements can be "closed" in the opening tag like this: <br />.

HTML5 does not require empty elements to be closed. But if you want stricter validation, or if you need to make your document readable by XML parsers, you must close all HTML elements properly.

HTML Headings

Headings are defined with the <h1> to <h6> tags.

<h1> defines the most important heading. <h6> defines the least important heading.

Example:

```
<h1>Heading 1</h1>

<h2>Heading 2</h2>

<h3>Heading 3</h3>

<h4>Heading 4</h4>

<h5>Heading 5</h5>

<h6>Heading 6</h6>
```

Browsers automatically add some white space (a margin) before and after a heading.

Headings are Important

Search engines use the headings to index the structure and content of your web pages.

Users often skim a page by its headings. It is important to use headings to show the document structure.

<h1> headings should be used for main headings, followed by <h2> headings, then the less important <h3>, and so on.

Use HTML headings for headings only. Don't use headings to make text BIG or bold.

Bigger Headings

Each HTML heading has a default size. However, you can specify the size for any heading with the style attribute, using the CSS font-size property:

Example:

```
<h1 style="font-size:60px;">Heading 1</h1>
```

HTML Horizontal Rules

The <hr> tag defines a thematic break in an HTML page, and is most often displayed as a horizontal rule.

The <hr> element is used to separate content (or define a change) in an HTML page:

Example:

```
<h1>This is heading 1</h1>

<p>This is some text.</p>

<hr>

<h2>This is heading 2</h2>

<p>This is some other text.</p>

<hr>
```

The HTML <head> Element

The HTML <head> element is a container for metadata. HTML metadata is data about the HTML document. Metadata is not displayed.

The <head> element is placed between the <html> tag and the <body> tag:

Example:

```
<!DOCTYPE html>

<html>

<head>

  <title>My First HTML</title>
```

```
<meta charset="UTF-8">

</head>

<body>

.

.

.
```

Note: Metadata typically define the document title, character set, styles, scripts, and other meta information.

Viewing HTML Source

- View HTML Source Code: Right-click in an HTML page and select "View Page Source" (in Chrome) or "View Source" (in Edge), or similar in other browsers. This will open a window containing the HTML source code of the page.

- Inspect an HTML Element: Right-click on an element (or a blank area), and choose "Inspect" or "Inspect Element" to see what elements are made up of (you will see both the HTML and the CSS). You can also edit the HTML or CSS on-the-fly in the Elements or Styles panel that opens.

- HTML Paragraphs: The HTML <p> element defines a paragraph.

Example:

```
<p>This is a paragraph.</p>

<p>This is another paragraph.</p>
```

Browsers automatically add some white space (a margin) before and after a paragraph.

HTML Display

You cannot be sure how HTML will be displayed. Large or small screens, and resized windows will create different results. With HTML, you cannot change the output by adding extra spaces or extra lines in your HTML code.

The browser will remove any extra spaces and extra lines when the page is displayed:

Example:

```
<p>

This paragraph

contains a lot of lines

in the source code,

but the browser
```

```
ignores it.
</p>
<p>
This paragraph
contains          a lot of spaces
in the source          code,
but the          browser
ignores it.
</p>
```

End Tag

Most browsers will display HTML correctly even if you forget the end tag:

Example:

```
<p>This is a paragraph.
<p>This is another paragraph.
```

The example above will work in most browsers, but do not rely on it.

Dropping the end tag can produce unexpected results or errors.

HTML Line Breaks

The HTML <br> element defines a line break.

Use <br> if you want a line break (a new line) without starting a new paragraph:

Example:

```
<p>This is<br>a paragraph<br>with line breaks.</p>
```

The <br> tag is an empty tag, which means that it has no end tag.

The Poem Problem

This poem will display on a single line.

Example:

```
<p>
 My Bonnie lies over the ocean.
 My Bonnie lies over the sea
```

```
   My Bonnie lies over the ocean.

   Oh, bring back my Bonnie to me.
</p>
```

The HTML <pre> Element

The HTML <pre> element defines preformatted text.

The text inside a <pre> element is displayed in a fixed-width font (usually Courier), and it preserves both spaces and line breaks:

Example:

```
<pre>
   My Bonnie lies over the ocean.

   My Bonnie lies over the sea.

   My Bonnie lies over the ocean.

   Oh, bring back my Bonnie to me.
</pre>
```

HTML Styles

Example:

| I am Red |

| I am Blue |

| I am Big |

The HTML Style Attribute

Setting the style of an HTML element, can be done with the style attribute.

The HTML style attribute has the following syntax:

```
<tagname style="property:value;">
```

The property is a CSS property. The value is a CSS value.

Background Color

The CSS background-color property defines the background color for an HTML element.

This example sets the background color for a page to powderblue.

Example:

```
<body style="background-color:powderblue;">
<h1>This is a heading</h1>
<p>This is a paragraph.</p>
</body>
```

Text Color

The CSS color property defines the text color for an HTML element:

Example:

```
<h1 style="color:blue;">This is a heading</h1>
<p style="color:red;">This is a paragraph.</p>
```

Fonts

The CSS font-family property defines the font to be used for an HTML element:

Example:

```
<h1 style="font-family:verdana;">This is a heading</h1>
<p style="font-family:courier;">This is a paragraph.</p>
```

Text Size

The CSS font-size property defines the text size for an HTML element:

Example:

```
<h1 style="font-size:300%;">This is a heading</h1>
<p style="font-size:160%;">This is a paragraph.</p>
```

Text Alignment

The CSS text-align property defines the horizontal text alignment for an HTML element:

Example:

```
<h1 style="text-align:center;">Centered Heading</h1>
<p style="text-align:center;">Centered paragraph.</p>
```

Text Formatting

| **This text is bold** |
| *This text is italic* |
| This is $_{subscript}$ and ^{superscript} |

HTML Formatting Elements

HTML also defines special elements for defining text with a special meaning.

HTML uses elements like <b> and <i> for formatting output, like bold or *italic* text.

Formatting elements were designed to display special types of text:

- <b> - Bold text
- <strong> - Important text
- <i> - Italic text
- <em> - Emphasized text
- <mark> - Marked text
- <small> - Small text
- <del> - Deleted text
- <ins> - Inserted text
- <sub> - Subscript text
- <sup> - Superscript text

HTML <b> and <strong> Elements

The HTML <b> element defines bold text, without any extra importance.

Example:

```
<b>This text is bold</b>
```

The HTML <strong> element defines strong text, with added semantic "strong" importance.

Example:

```
<strong>This text is strong</strong>
```

HTML <i> and <em> Elements

The HTML <i> element defines italic text, without any extra importance.

Example:

```
<i>This text is italic</i>
```

The HTML <em> element defines emphasized text, with added semantic importance.

Example:

```
<em>This text is emphasized</em>
```

Note: Browsers display <strong> as <b>, and <em> as <i>. However, there is a difference in the meaning of these tags: <b> and <i> defines bold and italic text, but <strong> and <em> means that the text is "important".

HTML <small> Element

The HTML <small> element defines smaller text:

Example:

```
<h2>HTML <small>Small</small> Formatting</h2>
```

HTML <mark> Element

The HTML <mark> element defines marked/highlighted text:

Example:

```
<h2>HTML <mark>Marked</mark> Formatting</h2>
```

HTML <del> Element

The HTML <del> element defines deleted/removed text.

Example:

```
<p>My favorite color is <del>blue</del> red.</p>
```

HTML <ins> Element

The HTML <ins> element defines inserted/added text.

Example:

```
<p>My favorite <ins>color</ins> is red.</p>
```

HTML <sub> Element

The HTML <sub> element defines subscripted text.

Example:

```
<p>This is <sub>subscripted</sub> text.</p>
```

HTML <sup> Element

The HTML <sup> element defines superscripted text.

Example:

```
<p>This is <sup>superscripted</sup> text.</p>
```

HTML Text Formatting Elements

Tag	Description
`<b>`	Defines bold text
`<em>`	Defines emphasized text
`<i>`	Defines italic text
`<small>`	Defines smaller text
`<strong>`	Defines important text
`<sub>`	Defines subscripted text
`<sup>`	Defines superscripted text
`<ins>`	Defines inserted text
`<del>`	Defines deleted text
`<mark>`	Defines marked/highlighted text

Hypertext Markup Language 5

HTML5 is the latest standard for browsers to display and interact with web pages.

The purpose of HTML5 is primarily to make it easier for web developers and browser creators to follow consensus-based standards that make compliance more efficient and empowering. It's also designed to provide better, faster, more consistent user experiences for desktop and mobile visitors.

For example, below is an HTML5 geolocation example from Building Your Startup with PHP: Geolocation and Google Places (Tuts+):

Here are a few key improvements in HTML5:

- There's a simpler, more straightforward element structure to pages, which makes them easier to build, adjust, and debug and to build automated services that help you find important resources on the web.

- It provides standard elements for commonplace media objects which previously required annoying plugins for audio, video, etc. These plugins needed to be regularly updated, i.e. repeated downloads to manage security.

- There's native integration with interfaces to leverage modern web and mobile needs. One of my favorite examples of this is geolocation, which allows you to determine the GPS co-ordinates of a web visitor through their browser. This feature was previously restricted to GPS-equipped phone apps.

Features of HTML5

HTML5 provides such an impressive list of new capabilities that the major browsers are still not fully compliant even 18 months after its acceptance.

There's also this interactive visual rainbow at HTML5 readiness. Hover over different arcs and you'll see which features are supported by which browsers.

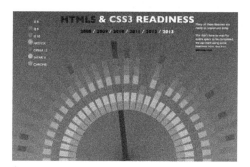

HTML5 Adoption Rates

Here's a visualization of the vastness of HTML5's capabilities.

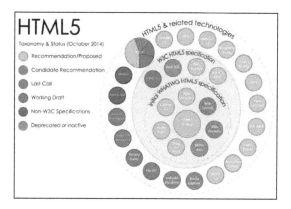

The New Elements of HTML5

The most basic new elements of HTML5 make it easier to lay out web pages and to debug your code or others'. It also makes it easier for automated services to scan the web and understand the importance of different page components.

For page layout and key features, there are now specific elements such as:

- <header> and <footer>.
- <nav> for all the kinds of menus.
- <aside> for sidebars or nearby related content.
- <article> where content goes such as a blog post.
- <section> similar to <div> but more content-oriented.
- <audio> and <video> tags to have native browsers manage playback of each. No more plugins and security updates for this.
- <canvas> specifically for letting you draw graphics on using a separate scripting language.
- <embed> to place external content or applications into the page.

Here are some of the more advanced features of HTML5, including API integration, making coding in JavaScript for sophisticated actions easier and more consistent across browsers:

- Audio and video playback: provides media playback across browsers without plugins.
- Geolocation: identify the location of the visitor.
- Drag and drop: for uploading files from the browser with simple gestures.
- Application cache: provides support for running HTML sites offline.
- Web workers: runs JavaScript in the background (non-blocking).
- Server sent events: allows servers to update web pages in a browser after they've been loaded, simpler and more efficient than AJAX and JavaScript.
- Offline data storage: provides a way to store data locally in the browser independent of cookies.

Applications of HTML5

Multimedia Elements

Using the <video>and <audio> HTML5 tags, we can add multimedia elements without using Adobe Flash or any other third-party plugin. All the action happens from the browser itself, which can help reduce the size of the final version file. For example, we can include product presentation videos, video reviews, podcasts, music samples, etc. The addition of these two tags expands the usage of HTML5.

Also, you can upload your videos to third-party sites like Vimeo or Youtube, and embed them in your new website. This is one of the most preferable options, because despite placing multimedia elements, the final size of your file is not affected.

Geolocation

Geolocation allows the site to detect the location of each user who enters the website. This can have various uses. For example, to offer language options depending on the user's location, improving the user experience.

It is a feature that requires user approval as it can compromise their privacy. This is why this option cannot be activated if the user does not approve it.

Applications

One of the main features of developing HTML5 applications is that the final result is completely accessible. That is, you can access this application from a computer, tablet or mobile phone. Even if you change devices, you can still access the web application via the respective URL, which is not the case with a mobile application.

Most web applications run from the cloud. A common example is mail clients like Gmail, which also have a mobile application.

Advantages

You don't need any special software to start programming in HTML5, you can even start programming in a notepad, save the document as HTML and view it from any browser. However, you can use a free code editor like Notepad+++, Atom, Eclipse, which offers basic functions like color differentiation between tags and content. It's really recommended to use a code editor instead of a text file, as it doesn't separate tags from content and can be more complicated to make corrections.

Structure

Through the incorporation of new tags such as: <header>, <section> or <footer>, among others, the HTML document can be structured in different parts, providing not only an appearance but also semantic content to our entire website.

HTML code can be easily separated between tags and content, allowing the developer to work more effectively and detect errors more quickly.

The tags are clear and descriptive, so the developer can start coding without any problems. It's really easy and simple language to understand in this new version.

Browser-Compatible

Modern and popular browsers such as Chrome, Firefox, Safari and Opera support HTML5. In other words, no matter which browser you use, the content can be viewed correctly. The only problem would be to consider users using older browsers, as not all new HTML5 functions and tags are available in those browsers.

You can check which HTML5 features each browser supports on the "Can I use" page and find out in advance if there are any features of your website that might be a problem in these past versions of browsers.

Adaptive Design

Any page made in HTML5 is compatible with both computers and mobile devices. In other words, you can set the mobile specification from the HTML document itself.

This is probably the most useful feature of the HTML5 language, because it allows users to access any web page or application from a mobile device as easily as they would from their computer.

References

- The-Most-Used-HTML-Tags, what-is-html: hostinger.in, Retrieved 8 July, 2019

- Html-elements, html: w3schools.com, Retrieved 12 April, 2019

- What-is-html5--cms-25803: tutsplus.com, Retrieved 21 June, 2019

- What-is-html5-and-what-can-i-do-with-it-d6bc85eb8af9: medium.com, Retrieved 25 August, 2019

- Difference-between-html-and-html5: hostinger.com, Retrieved 2 May, 2019

JavaScript

JavaScript refers to a high-level, interpreted scripting language which conforms to the ECMAScript specification. It can support functional, imperative and event-driven programming styles. Some of the popular JavaScript frameworks are AngularJS, ReactJS, MeteorJS and jQuery. The diverse applications of these JavaScript frameworks have been thoroughly discussed in this chapter.

JavaScript is a high level, interpreted, programming language used to make web pages more interactive.

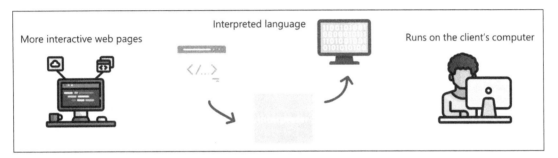

JavaScript is the language of the web, it is used to make the web look alive by adding motion to it. To be more precise, it's a programming language that let's you implement complex and beautiful things/design on web pages. When you notice a web page doing more than just sit there and gawk at you, you can bet that the web page is using JavaScript.

Feature of JavaScript

- Scripting language and not Java: In fact, JavaScript has nothing to do with Java. Then why is it called "Java" Script? When JavaScript was first released it was called Mocha, it was later renamed to LiveScript and then to JavaScript when Netscape (founded JavaScript) and Sun did a license agreement.

- Object-based scripting language which supports polymorphism, encapsulation and to some extent inheritance as well.

- Interpreted language: It doesn't have to be compiled like Java and C which require a compiler.

- JavaScript runs in a browser: You can run it on Google Chrome, Internet Explorer, Safari, etc. JavaScript can execute not only in the browser but also on the server and any device which has a JavaScript Engine.

Currently, we have 100s of programming languages and every day new languages are being created. Among these are few powerful languages that bring about big changes in the market and JavaScript is one of them.

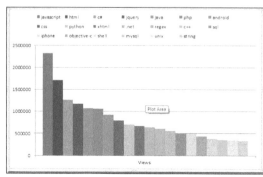

Stack overflow stats

JavaScript has always been on the list of popular programming languages. According to Stack-Overflow, for the 6th year in a row, JavaScript has remained the most popular and commonly used programming language.

- JavaScript is mainly known for creating beautiful web pages & applications. An example of this is Google Maps. If you want to explore a specific map, all you have to do is click and drag with the mouse. And what sort of language could do that? You guessed it. It's JavaScript.

- JavaScript can also be used in smart watches. An example of this is the popular smart-watch maker called Pebble. Pebble has created Pebble.js which is a small JavaScript framework that allows a developer to create an application for the Pebble line of watches in JavaScript.

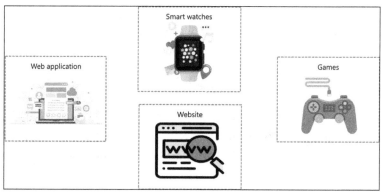

Applications of JavaScript

- Most popular websites like Google, Facebook, Netflix, Amazon, etc make use of JavaScript to build their websites.

- Among things like mobile applications, digital art, web servers and server applications, JavaScript is also used to make Games. A lot of developers are building small-scale games and apps using JavaScript.

HTML, CSS and JavaScript

Anyone familiar with JavaScript knows that it has something to do with HTML and CSS. But what is the relationship between these three?

HTML, CSS and JavaScript

Think of HTML (HyperText Markup Language) as the skeleton of the web. It is used for displaying the web.

On the other hand, CSS is like our clothes. We put on fashionable clothes to look better. Similarly, the web is quite stylish as well. It uses CSS which stands for Cascading Style Sheets for styling purpose.

Then there is JavaScript which puts life into a web page. Just like how kids move around using the skateboard, the web also motions with the help of JavaScript.

Benefits of JavaScript

There has to be a reason why so many developers love working on JavaScript. Well, there are several benefits of using JavaScript for developing web applications, here's a few benefits:

1. It's easy to learn and simple to implement. It is a weak-type programming language unlike the strong-type programming languages like Java and C++, which have strict rules for coding.

2. It's all about being fast in today's world and since JavaScript is mainly a client-side programming language, it is very fast because any code can run immediately instead of having to contact the server and wait for an answer.

3. Rich set of frameworks like AngularJS, ReactJS are used to build web applications and perform different tasks.

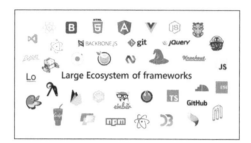

4. Builds interactive websites: We all get attracted to beautifully designed websites and JavaScript is the reason behind such attractive websites and applications.

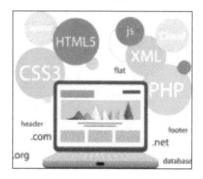

5. JavaScript is an interpreted language that does not require a compiler because the web interprets JavaScript. All you need is a browser like Google chrome or internet explorer and you can do all sorts of stuff in the browser.

6. JavaScript is platform independent and it is supported by all major browsers like Internet Explorer, Google Chrome, Mozilla Firefox, Safari, etc.

JavaScript Fundamentals

1. Variables

2. Constants

3. Data Types

4. Objects

5. Arrays

6. Functions

7. Conditional statements

8. Loops

9. Switch case.

Variables

Variable is a name given to a memory location which acts as a container for storing data temporarily. They are nothing but reserved memory locations to store values.

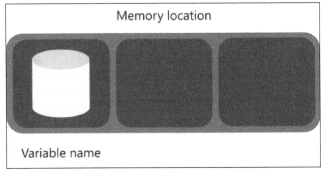

Variables

To declare a variable in JavaScript use the 'let' keyword. For example:

```
1. let age;
2. age=22;
```

In the above example, we've declared a variable 'age' by using the 'let' keyword and then we've stored a value (22) in it. So here a memory location is assigned to the 'age' variable and it contains a value i.e. '22'.

Constants

Constants are fixed values that don't change during execution time. To declare a constant in JavaScript use the 'const' keyword.

For example:

```
const mybirthday;

mybirthday='3rd August'.
```

Data Types

You can assign different types of values to a variable such as a number or a string. In JavaScript, there are two categories of data types:

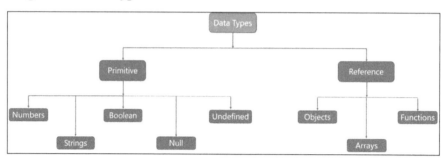

Data Types

Objects

An object is a stand alone entity with properties and types and it is a lot like an object in real life. For example, consider a girl, whose name is Emily, age is 22 and eye-color is brown. In this example the object is the girl and her name, age and eye-color are her properties.

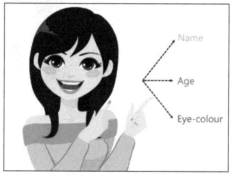

Objects example

Objects are variables too, but they contain many values, so instead of declaring different variables for each property, you can declare an object which stores all these properties.

To declare an object in JavaScript use the 'let' keyword and make sure to use curly brackets in such a way that all property-value pairs are defined within the curly brackets. For example:

```
let girl= {

name: 'Emily',

age: 22,

eyeColour: 'Brown'

};
```

In the above example, we've declared an object called 'girl' and it has 3 properties (name, age, eye colour) with values (Emily, 22, Brown).

Arrays

An array is a data structure that contains a list of elements which store multiple values in a single variable.

For example, let's consider a scenario where you went shopping to buy art supplies. The list of items you bought can be put into an array.

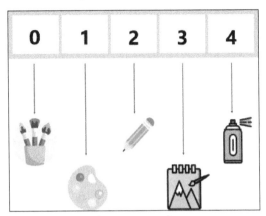

Arrays example

To declare an array in JavaScript use the 'let' keyword with square brackets and all the array elements must be enclosed within them.

For example:

```
let shopping=[];

shopping=['paintBrush','sprayPaint','waterColours','canvas'];
```

In the above example we've declared an array called 'shopping' and we've added four elements in it.

Also, array elements are numbered from zero. For example this is how you access the first array element:

```
shopping[0];
```

Functions

A function is a block of organised, reusable code that is used to perform single, related action.

Let's create a function that calculates the product of two numbers.

To declare a function in JavaScript use the 'function' keyword. For example:

```
function product(a, b) {

return a*b;

}
```

In the above example, we've declared a function called 'product' and we've passed 2 parameters to this function, 'a' and 'b' which are variables whose product is returned by this function. Now, in order to call a function and pass a value to these parameters you'll have to follow the below syntax:

```
product(8,2);
```

In the above code snippet we're calling the product function with a set of values (8 & 2). These are values of the variables 'a' and 'b' and they're called as arguments to the function.

Conditional Statements – if

Conditional statement is a set of rules performed if a certain condition is met. The 'if' statement is used to execute a block of code, only if the condition specified holds true.

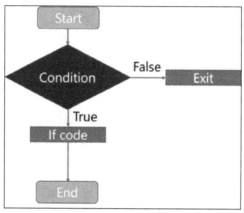

if flowchart

To declare an if statement in JavaScript use the 'if' keyword. The syntax is:

```
if(condition) {

statement;

}
```

Now let's look at an example:

```
let numbers=[1,2,1,2,3,2,3,1];

if(numbers[0]==numbers[2]) {

console.log('Correct!');

}
```

In the above example we've defined an array of numbers and then we've defined an if block. Within this block is a condition and a statement. The condition is '(numbers[0]==numbers[2])' and the statement is 'console.log('Correct!')'. If the condition is met, only then the statement will be executed.

Conditional Statements- Else if

Else statement is used to execute a block of code if the same condition is false.

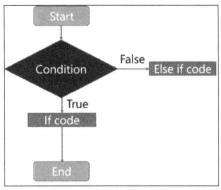

Else if flowchart

The syntax is:

```
if(condition) {

statement a;

}

else (condition) {

statement b;

}
```

Now let's look at an example:

```
let numbers=[1,2,1,2,3,2,3,1];

if(numbers[0]==numbers[4] {

console.log("Correct!");

}

else {

console.log("Wrong, please try again");

}
```

In the above example, we've defined an if block as well as an else block. So if the conditions within the if block holds false then the else block gets executed.

Loops

Loops are used to repeat a specific block until some end condition is met. There are three categories of loops in JavaScript:

1. While loop

2. Do-while loop

3. For loop.

While Loop

While the condition is true, the code within the loop is executed.

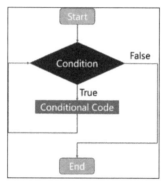

While loop flowchart

The syntax is:

```
while(condition) {
loop code;
}
```

Now let's look at an example:

```
let i=0;
while(i < 5) {
console.log("The number is " +i);
i++;
}
```

In the above example, we've defined a while loop wherein we've set a condition. As long as the condition holds true, the while loop is executed.

Do While Loop

This loop will first execute the code, then check the condition and while the condition holds true, execute repeatedly.

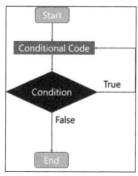

Do while loop flowchart

Refer the syntax to better understand it:

```
do {
loop code;
} while (condition);
```

This loop executes the code block once before checking if the condition is true, then it will repeat the loop as long as the condition holds true.

Now let's look at an example:

```
do {
console.log ("The number is " +i);
i++;
}
while (i > 5);
```

The above code is similar to the while loop code except, the code block within the do loop is first executed and only then the condition within the while loop is checked. If the condition holds true then the do loop is executed again.

For Loop

The for loop repeatedly executes the loop code while a given condition is TRUE. It tests the condition before executing the loop body.

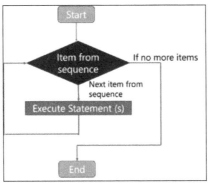

For loop flowchart

The syntax is:

```
for (begin; condition; step) {
loop code;
}
```

In the above syntax:

- Begin statement is executed one time before the execution of the loop code.

- Condition defines the condition for executing the loop code.

- Step statement is executed every time after the code block has been executed.

For example:

```
for (i=0;i<5;i++) {
console.log("The number is " +i);
}
```

In the above example, we've defined a for loop within which we've defined the begin, condition and step statements. The begin statement is that 'i=0'. After executing the begin statement the code within the for loop is executed one time. Next, the condition is checked, if 'i<5' then, the code within the loop is executed. After this, the last step statement (i++) is executed.

Switch Case

The switch statement is used to perform different actions based on different conditions.

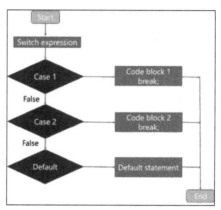

Switch case flowchart

Let's look at the syntax for switch case:

```
switch(expression) {
case 1:
code block 1
break;
case 2:
code block 2
break;
default:
code block 3
break;
}
```

How does it work?

- Switch expression gets evaluated once,
- Value of the expression is compared with the values of each case,
- If there is a match, the associated block of code is executed.

Let's try this with an example:

```
let games='football';

switch(games) {

case "throwball":

console.log("I dislike throwball!");

break;

case "football":

console.log("I love football!");

break;

case "cricket":

console.log("I'm a huge cricket fan!");

break;

default:

console.log("I like other games");

break;

}
```

In the above example the switch expression is 'games' and the value of games is 'football'. The value of 'games' is compared with the value of each case. In this example it is compared to 'throwball', 'cricket' and 'football'. The value of 'games' matches with the case 'football', therefore the code within the 'football' case is executed.

Advantages of JavaScript

The merits of using JavaScript are:

- Less server interaction: You can validate user input before sending the page off to the server. This saves server traffic, which means less load on your server.

- Immediate feedback to the visitors: They don't have to wait for a page reload to see if they have forgotten to enter something.

- Increased interactivity: You can create interfaces that react when the user hovers over them with a mouse or activates them via the keyboard.

- Richer interfaces: You can use JavaScript to include such items as drag-and-drop components and sliders to give a Rich Interface to your site visitors.

Limitations of JavaScript

We cannot treat JavaScript as a full-fledged programming language. It lacks the following important features:

- Client-side JavaScript does not allow the reading or writing of files. This has been kept for security reason.

- JavaScript cannot be used for networking applications because there is no such support available.

- JavaScript doesn't have any multi-threading or multiprocessor capabilities.

Once again, JavaScript is a lightweight, interpreted programming language that allows you to build interactivity into otherwise static HTML pages.

JavaScript Development Tools

One of major strengths of JavaScript is that it does not require expensive development tools. You can start with a simple text editor such as Notepad. Since it is an interpreted language inside the context of a web browser, you don't even need to buy a compiler.

To make our life simpler, various vendors have come up with very nice JavaScript editing tools. Some of them are listed here:

- Microsoft FrontPage: Microsoft has developed a popular HTML editor called FrontPage. FrontPage also provides web developers with a number of JavaScript tools to assist in the creation of interactive websites.

- Macromedia Dreamweaver MX: Macromedia Dreamweaver MX is a very popular HTML and JavaScript editor in the professional web development crowd. It provides several handy prebuilt JavaScript components, integrates well with databases, and conforms to new standards such as XHTML and XML.

- Macromedia HomeSite 5: HomeSite 5 is a well-liked HTML and JavaScript editor from Macromedia that can be used to manage personal websites effectively.

Client-side JavaScript

Client-side JavaScript is the most common form of the language. The script should be included in or referenced by an HTML document for the code to be interpreted by the browser.

It means that a web page need not be a static HTML, but can include programs that interact with the user, control the browser, and dynamically create HTML content.

The JavaScript client-side mechanism provides many advantages over traditional CGI server-side scripts. For example, you might use JavaScript to check if the user has entered a valid e-mail address in a form field.

The JavaScript code is executed when the user submits the form, and only if all the entries are valid, they would be submitted to the web server.

JavaScript can be used to trap user-initiated events such as button clicks, link navigation, and other actions that the user initiates explicitly or implicitly.

JavaScript Frameworks

AngularJS

AngularJS is a JavaScript framework that operates on the client side and is used to develop web applications.

This means that the code you write will be executed by the browser and not by the server. It is a popular and powerful JavaScript framework and is widely used in single page application projects and line of business applications.

Due to this, various AngularJs application development companies are in demand now.

Web development is one of the most preferred and cost-effective ways to create distributed applications.

The deployment done once on one machine can be made accessible to all the users on the world wide web. One of the performance issues that came up was the page posting issue which resulted in communication lag between the client and the server.

AngularJS was developed by Misko and Adam Abrons in 2009 in order to help combat such issues and is being maintained by Google since then. It is an open source project which means you can freely use and share it.

AngularJS Architecture

AngularJS follows the MVC architecture, the diagram of the MVC framework as shown below.

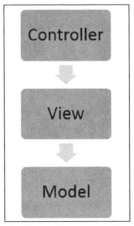

AngularJS Architecture Diagram

- The Controller represents the layer that has the business logic. User events trigger the functions which are stored inside your controller. The user events are part of the controller.

- Views are used to represent the presentation layer which is provided to the end users.

- Models are used to represent your data. The data in your model can be as simple as just having primitive declarations. For example, if you are maintaining a student application, your data model could just have a student id and a name. Or it can also be complex by having a structured data model. If you are maintaining a car ownership application, you can have structures to define the vehicle itself in terms of its engine capacity, seating capacity, etc.

Advantages of AngularJS

Dependency Injection

In software engineering, dependency injection refers to the passing of objects between the application and the client.

Injection is the phenomenon of passing a dependency (say an application service) to a dependent object (say a client) that would use it. AngularJS provides several core components for achieving this purpose in simplicity.

Model View Controller

AngularJS is used to create Rich Internet Applications (RIA), and two-way data binding is achievable due to the MVC (model view controller) architecture in Angular JS.

A basic depiction of this architecture is as shown below:

MVC Model for AngularJS

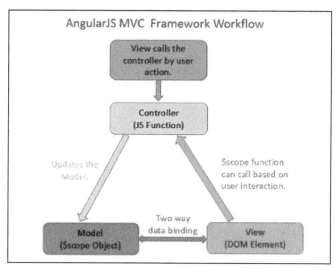

As developers, we just have to split our code into the model, view, and controller and the rest of the operations such as managing the components and connecting them together will be automatically done by AngularJS.

Two-way Data Binding

Software changes should be responsive, and changes within the system should be catered to the changes in the user interface and conversely, with precision and speed.

AngularJS offers this kind of binding by synchronizing between the model and the view.

Testing

It is interesting to know the fact that AngularJS was designed keeping testing in mind, right from the beginning.

Any of the components of AngularJS can be comfortably tested using both unit testing and an end to end testing. The application can be transported across browsers for testing purposes.

Controlling the Behavior of DOM Elements

Attributes of AngularJS can be linked to directives so that automatic initialization of the application is possible.

This means that there is modularity in AngularJS and with the help of its features such as directives and filters, a sense of customization and flexibility can be achieved in the code.

It is always better to learn a technological trend and keep updating ourselves often to make the most out of our careers and also to keep that inquisitive mind of ours always thirsty for knowledge.

Pre-requisites for Learning AngularJS

It is important and advantageous to know a few things in advance to speed up your learning pace.

HTML and CSS could be used to build your own web pages so that testing can be done on them. To code in AngularJS, it is important to have a basic understanding of JavaScript.

Hence, it is advisable to get a basic understanding of HTML and CSS along with the concepts of implementing JavaScript, before starting off with AngularJS.

Features of AngularJS

In AngularJS language there are many offerings that are unique and exclusive. It is better to get yourself acquainted to these before setting up an environment to write and execute the code in AngularJS.

MVC Architecture

Model-view-controller design of AngularJS has to be understood, for understanding how the code works.

MVC forms the core of this programming language and hence is very important too. Whenever an event occurs, the controller part of the codebase receives the input of the event which consists of varied requests for the application.

The model part of the codebase, which usually is the core logic, coordinates with the controller and prepares the required data that has to be used by the view to generate a presentable output. Hence there is a separation of concerns within the programming language architecture as it isolates the application logic from the UI layer.

This is the reason for which AngularJS is widely used in developing Single Page Applications (SPA).

Directives

AngularJS is integrated with the HTML code to create web pages, and "Directives" are the special attributes of AngularJS and are used in order to integrate them.

Expressions in AngularJS

AngularJS expressions can contain literals, operators or variables, unlike the traditional JavaScript.

They could be written inside the HTML tag itself, but care has to be taken to add the ng-app directive, else the expression will be displayed as it is, without being solved.

AngularJS expressions could be written inside double curly braces or can be written inside a directive.

Syntax

Inside curly braces:

```
<div ng-app="">
<p>My first expression in Angular JS: {{3+3}}</p>
</div>
```

Inside directive:

```
<div ng-controller="Name of your controller">
<element ng-bind="your expression"></element>
</div>
```

AngularJS Numbers

This datatype is just like the JavaScript datatype and operators could be used to display results.

Example:

```
<div ng-app="">
<p>The value of 5 times 10 is : {{5*10}}<p>
</div>
```

AngularJS Strings

Strings can be initialized using ng-init directive or ng-controller directive. The concatenation of strings is also possible when the + operator is used within the expression.

Strings also could be used as expressions within double curly braces or use ng-bind directive just like the AngularJS numbers.

Syntax

Inside curly braces:

```
<div ng-app="" ng-init="first string variable name='your first string';second string variable name

='your second string'">

<p>My first string expression in Angular JS:

{{ first string variable name + second string variable name }}</p>

</div>
```

Inside directive:

```
<div ng-app="" ng-init=" first string variable name='your first string';

second string variable name='your second string'">

<p>My first string expression in Angular JS:<span ng-bind=

" first string variable name + second string variable name "></span></p>

</div>
```

AngularJS Objects

AngularJS objects behave the same way in which the JavaScript objects behave. The items within an object could be accessed using the dot operator.

Syntax

Inside curly braces:

```
<div ng-app="" ng-init="your object name=

{first variable name='your first value',second variable name

='your second value'}">

<p>My first object in Angular JS: {{ your object name.second variable name }}</p>

</div>
```

Inside directive:

```
<div ng-app="" ng-init="your object name={first variable name='your first val-
ue',second variable name
```

```
='your second value'}">

<p>My first object in Angular JS:<span ng-bind=" your object name.second variable
name "></span></p>

</div>
```

AngularJS Arrays

AngularJS arrays behave the same way in which the JavaScript arrays behave.

The items within an array could be accessed by denoting the value's index number within square braces. Please remember that the indexing starts from zero always, in an array, i.e., Array element 1 = index 0.

Array element 2 = index 1 and so on.

Syntax

Inside curly braces:

```
<div ng-app="" ng-init="your array name=[your first value,your second value]">

<p>My first array in Angular JS: {{ your array name[1] }}</p>

</div>
```

Inside directive:

```
<div ng-app="" ng-init="your array name=[your first value,your second value]">

<p>My first array in Angular JS: <span ng-bind="your array name[1] "></span></p>

</div>
```

A code snippet Example showing all the expressions in AngularJS is given below:

Please Note and AngularJS

- Does not support conditionals, loops, and exceptions in expressions.

- Does not support function declaration (even inside the ng-init directive) in expressions.

- Does not support bitwise, comma, void and new operator in expressions.

- Ignores the null or undefined properties in expressions.

- Expressions are evaluated belonging to the scope object and not the global window.

AngularJS Filters

Filters are exclusive to AngularJS and are not present in the traditional JavaScript.

The filters are used to modify output data to make them compatible with different input data. The filters could be used in expressions or directives with the help of the pipe operator.

These are the different kind of filters which are commonly used:

- Uppercase: Helps to format the strings into uppercase.

Syntax

```
<div ng-app="" ng-controller="first string variable name">

<p>My first string expression in uppercase in Angular JS:

{{ first string variable name | uppercase}}</p>

</div>
```

- Lowercase: Helps to format the strings into lowercase.

Syntax

```
<div ng-app="" ng-controller="first string variable name">

<p>My first string expression in lowercase in AngularJS:

{{ first string variable name | lowercase}}</p>

</div>
```

- Currency: This filter is used on number expressions to convert them and display in terms of currency. Pipe operator could be used along with the number of expressions for this conversion.

Syntax

```
<div ng-app="" ng-init="your number value">

<h1>Price : {{ your number value | currency }}</h1>

 </div>
```

- Filter: This can be used only on arrays to select a subset of an array.

Syntax

```
<div ng-app="" ng-controller="your array name">

<ul>

<li ng-repeat="x in your array name | filter: 'i'">

{{x}}

</li>

</ul>

</div>
```

- OrderBy: This filter can be added to directives such as ng-repeat to display them in order. Pipe operator can be used with the ng-repeat in unordered lists to achieve this.

Syntax

```
<div ng-app="" ng-controller="your object name">

<ul>

<li ng-repeat="x in your object name | orderBy:'your desired order'">

{{x.your first variable+x.your second variable}}

</li>

</ul>

</div>
```

The code examples below show all the filters being used:

Disadvantages of AngularJS

Though AngularJS comes with a lot of merits, here are some points of concern:

- Not Secure: Being JavaScript only framework, application written in AngularJS are not safe. Server side authentication and authorization is must to keep an application secure.

- Not degradable: If the user of your application disables JavaScript, then nothing would be visible, except the basic page.

AngularJS Directives

The AngularJS framework can be divided into three major parts:

- Ng-app: This directive defines and links an AngularJS application to HTML.

- Ng-model: This directive binds the values of AngularJS application data to HTML input controls.

- Ng-bind: This directive binds the AngularJS application data to HTML tags.

ReactJS

JavaScript programming is widely used to develop web applications as it is a lightweight language that is supported by all browsers. It supports the procedural and object-oriented languages, so it is used to create client-side scripts to make dynamic web-pages.

Many frameworks can be used with JavaScript depending on the project requirements and React framework is one of them. JavaScript is one of the most preferred scripting languages used by the web designers and it offers the following features to web projects:

- Security

- Efficiency

- Cost Reduction

React is giving a neck to neck competition to Angular that is a quite older framework for JavaScript due to its array of features. The main reason behind the popularity of ReactJS is the way in which data flow takes place. Earlier the frameworks were using the traditional approach in which the web pages need to be refreshed to check any update.

Web pages can receive data from any source like real-time data, user input data, or initial data that can be dispatched by any dispatcher. After fetching data, it is usually forwarded to the store that transfers it to view. Through view, you or any other user can interact with the web application, so web pages come in view category of MVC architecture.

Do you know that in this traditional approach every time new data is added at the back end? At the time when the browser gets updates only then the user can see the new data on the view. This complete update cycle is handled by DOM or Document Object Model that is created by the browser when the web page is loaded or refreshed and it can dynamically add or remove data to and from the web page. Though Dom creation is done dynamically, this is memory wastage and degrades the overall application performance too.

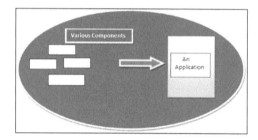

As the Dom creation process was costly and inefficient, so a new technology was needed to save time and resources. ReactJS is proved such an efficient technology, that provides a new way to perform this task of handling views at the client side. Through ReactJS, a single application can be divided into many components, same traditional data flow technique is used in ReactJS, but at the back end, the way to handle data has been changed.

In ReactJS, when data gets the update it does not reload the full web page, instead, it reloads a portion of the web page and updates only selected component that was changed. Moreover, ReactJS uses virtual DOM instead of DOM to save the memory space.

ReactJS is not a framework instead is a component-based library that was introduced by the Facebook. Now it is one of the most popular JavaScript libraries with a strong foundation and large supportive community. In ReactJS, everything is just like a component that is taken as the basic building blocks of the application.

Here, the use of component makes ReactJS an efficient library collection as they are easy to handle, one can change just a single component when it is required rather than changing the complete page layout. For real-time or large sized applications, this feature is quite important. In ReactJS, component states get changed when they are updated. As a result, the whole page need not be reloaded when the application gets changed.

This library was developed by Facebook's software engineer Jordan Walke and initially, Facebook implemented ReactJS in its news feed in 2011, while by 2013 it was made available for every user. Use of ReactJS made Facebook more popular and many users get satisfied by this. Now any of the JavaScript users can use this set of the library that was initially used only by the Facebook.

Significance of ReactJS

Virtual DOM

Just like real DOM, virtual DOM is also a node tree in which elements, their attributes, and content work as objects and properties. In React, a node tree is created by the render function in which all components of React are used. This tree gets updated as per the changes of components either by the user or system, this rotation is called mutation. Tree mutation is performed in these three simple steps:

1. On changing of any underlying data complete UI is re-rendered virtually.

2. Difference between current and previous DOM is calculated.

3. As per result of the calculation, DOM gets changed.

These changes are applied to a certain part of the application, rather than complete application and so application becomes faster and less memory gets wasted.

Use of JSX

JSX stands for JavaScript XML. For JSX files, 'react' uses HTML/XML like syntaxes, that can be used by Babel-like pre-processors and through that HTML like syntaxes can be transformed easily to Java objects. Through JSX after conversion to JavaScript objects, again the code can be embedded inside JavaScript. These JSX files make the HTML code easy to understand and help in boosting the overall application performance too. Applications become robust due to these files.

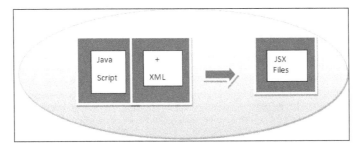

Testability

ReactJS makes an application testable and it is easy to debug and test. It uses views that can be used as the states of the functions. Component states can be easily manipulated and passed to the ReactJS view, where the action, function, and event can be easily checked and tested. ReactJS has improved application quality by providing feature rich libraries.

Simplicity

ReactJS JSX files are really easy and simple to understand. The user can quickly code and understand JSX files. Though plain JavaScript can also be used here, it is quite easier to use JSX files. As it is a component-based library, in which each component has a separate life cycle, so it is easier to use ReactJS.

Low Learning Curve

ReactJS learning curve is low and easier. Anyone who has even basic programming knowledge can learn and use ReactJS. So, even if you have basic programming skills and know how to code in HTML and JavaScript, then you can learn ReactJS quickly.

One-way Data Binding

In ReactJS, uni-directional data flow is used that is also called data binding. Here, application states are kept in specific stores and therefore rest of the components remain loosely coupled and as a result application becomes more flexible and efficient.

Basic Building Blocks of ReactJS

However, anyone who has a little bit knowledge of HTML, but still it is good to know the basic building blocks of ReactJS so that you can design and use the application as per your requirements. ReactJS treats everything as a component that may have certain specific props, state, and lifecycle and so on. So, in short, we can say that ReactJS has following building blocks:

- Components: An application consists of many components that are used to serve different purposes. This way we can keep the view and logic separate. These ReactJS components can either be stateful or stateless. While defining components, we firstly import react-dom libraries and then we can code for the component.

- Properties or Props: Props is used by React components to pass parent properties to child components. These are like arguments that are passed to the ReactJS functions or components that are then processed by the React.

- State: States helps to create interactive and dynamic components. Generally, it is used with data that changes frequently. Like a button or property can be in the active or inactive state, we can use it through render function and can be set inside constructors.

- Event Handling or State Manipulation: Events like the click of button or mouse hovering may require some action. Event handlers are used to handle such events. Initially, the component state can be set in constructors, but if required, these states can be manipulated by using the setState command. Moreover, the IsToggleOn function can switch the state from active to inactive or vice versa.

- State Lifecycle: As component requirements, resources need to be initialized. This initialization of resources is called "mounting". Mounting and un-mounting of resources can be done by the ReactJS easily and for this, there are ready to use functions available in the React framework.

ReactJS - State

State is the place where the data comes from. We should always try to make our state as simple as possible and minimize the number of stateful components. If we have, for example, ten components that need data from the state, we should create one container component that will keep the state for all of them.

Using State

The following sample code shows how to create a stateful component using EcmaScript 2016 syntax.

App.jsx

```
import React from 'react';
class App extends React.Component {
    constructor(props) {
```

```
        super(props);


        this.state = {
            header: "Header from state...",
            content: "Content from state..."
        }
    }
    render() {
        return (
            <div>
                <h1>{this.state.header}</h1>
                <h2>{this.state.content}</h2>
            </div>
        );
    }
}
export default App;
```

Main.JS

```
import React from 'react';
import ReactDOM from 'react-dom';
import App from './App.jsx';


ReactDOM.render(<App />, document.getElementById('app'));
```

This will produce the following result.

ReactJS Props

The main difference between state and props is that props are immutable. This is why the container component should define the state that can be updated and changed, while the child components should only pass data from the state using props.

Using Props

When we need immutable data in our component, we can just add props to reactdom.render() function in main.js and use it inside our component.

App.jsx

```
import React from 'react';


class App extends React.Component {

   render() {

      return (

         <div>

            <h1>{this.props.headerProp}</h1>

            <h2>{this.props.contentProp}</h2>

         </div>

      );

   }

}

export default App;
```

Main.js

```
import React from 'react';

import ReactDOM from 'react-dom';

import App from './App.jsx';


ReactDOM.render(<App headerProp = "Header from props..." contentProp = "Content
   from props..."/>, document.getElementById('app'));


export default App;
```

This will produce the following result-

Default Props

You can also set default property values directly on the component constructor instead of adding it to the reactdom.render() element.

App.jsx

```
import React from 'react';


class App extends React.Component {

    render() {

        return (

            <div>

                <h1>{this.props.headerProp}</h1>

                <h2>{this.props.contentProp}</h2>

            </div>

        );

    }

}
App.defaultProps = {

    headerProp: "Header from props...",

    contentProp:"Content from props..."

}

export default App;
```

main.js

```
import React from 'react';
```

```
import ReactDOM from 'react-dom';

import App from './App.jsx';


ReactDOM.render(<App/>, document.getElementById('app'));
```

Output is the same as before.

State and Props

The following example shows how to combine state and props in your app. We are setting the state in our parent component and passing it down the component tree using props. Inside the render function, we are setting headerprop and contentprop used in child components.

App.jsx

```
import React from 'react';


class App extends React.Component {
    constructor(props) {
        super(props);
        this.state = {
            header: "Header from props...",
            content: "Content from props..."
        }
    }
    render() {
        return (
            <div>
                <Header headerProp = {this.state.header}/>
                <Content contentProp = {this.state.content}/>
```

```
            </div>
        );
    }
}
class Header extends React.Component {
    render() {
        return (
            <div>
                <h1>{this.props.headerProp}</h1>
            </div>
        );
    }
}
class Content extends React.Component {
    render() {
        return (
            <div>
                <h2>{this.props.contentProp}</h2>
            </div>
        );
    }
}
export default App;
```

Main.JS

```
import React from 'react';
import ReactDOM from 'react-dom';
import App from './App.jsx';


ReactDOM.render(<App/>, document.getElementById('app'));
```

The result will again be the same as in the previous two examples, the only thing that is different is the source of our data, which is now originally coming from the state. When we want to update it, we just need to update the state, and all child components will be updated.

ReactJS - Props Validation

Properties validation is a useful way to force the correct usage of the components. This will help during development to avoid future bugs and problems, once the app becomes larger. It also makes the code more readable, since we can see how each component should be used.

Validating Props

In this example, we are creating App component with all the props that we need. App.propTypes is used for props validation. If some of the props aren't using the correct type that we assigned, we will get a console warning. After we specify validation patterns, we will set app.defaultProps.

App.jsx

```
import React from 'react';


class App extends React.Component {
   render() {
      return (
         <div>
            <h3>Array: {this.props.propArray}</h3>
            <h3>Bool: {this.props.propBool ? "True..." : "False..."}</h3>
            <h3>Func: {this.props.propFunc(3)}</h3>
            <h3>Number: {this.props.propNumber}</h3>
            <h3>String: {this.props.propString}</h3>
            <h3>Object: {this.props.propObject.objectName1}</h3>
            <h3>Object: {this.props.propObject.objectName2}</h3>
            <h3>Object: {this.props.propObject.objectName3}</h3>
         </div>
      );
```

```
    }
}


App.propTypes = {
    propArray: React.PropTypes.array.isRequired,
    propBool: React.PropTypes.bool.isRequired,
    propFunc: React.PropTypes.func,
    propNumber: React.PropTypes.number,
    propString: React.PropTypes.string,
    propObject: React.PropTypes.object
}


App.defaultProps = {
    propArray: [1,2,3,4,5],
    propBool: true,
    propFunc: function(e){return e},
    propNumber: 1,
    propString: "String value...",

    propObject: {
        objectName1:"objectValue1",
        objectName2: "objectValue2",
        objectName3: "objectValue3"
    }
}
export default App;
```

Main.JS

```
import React from 'react';
import ReactDOM from 'react-dom';
import App from './App.jsx';


ReactDOM.render(<App/>, document.getElementById('app'));
```

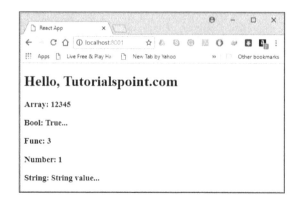

ReactJS - Component API

We will discuss three methods: setState(), forceUpdate and ReactDOM.findDOMNode(). In new ES6 classes, we have to manually bind this. We will use this.method.bind(this) in the examples.

Set State

setState() method is used to update the state of the component. This method will not replace the state, but only add changes to the original state.

```
import React from 'react';


class App extends React.Component {
   constructor() {
      super();


      this.state = {
         data: []
      }


      this.setStateHandler = this.setStateHandler.bind(this);
   };
   setStateHandler() {
      var item = "setState...";
      var myArray = this.state.data.slice();
         myArray.push(item);
      this.setState({data: myArray})
```

```
};
    render() {
        return (
            <div>
                <button onClick = {this.setStateHandler}>SET STATE</button>
                <h4>State Array: {this.state.data}</h4>
            </div>
        );
    }
}
export default App;
```

We started with an empty array. Every time we click the button, the state will be updated. If we click five times, we will get the following output.

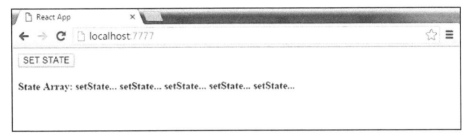

Force Update

Sometimes we might want to update the component manually. This can be achieved using the forceUpdate() method.

```
import React from 'react';


class App extends React.Component {
    constructor() {
        super();
        this.forceUpdateHandler = this.forceUpdateHandler.bind(this);
    };
    forceUpdateHandler() {
        this.forceUpdate();
    };
```

```
    render() {

        return (

            <div>

                <button onClick = {this.forceUpdateHandler}>FORCE UPDATE</button>

                <h4>Random number: {Math.random()}</h4>

            </div>

        );

    }

}

export default App;
```

We are setting a random number that will be updated every time the button is clicked.

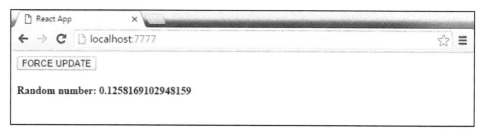

Find Dom Node

For DOM manipulation, we can use ReactDOM.findDOMNode() method. First we need to import react-dom.

```
import React from 'react';

import ReactDOM from 'react-dom';


class App extends React.Component {

    constructor() {

        super();

        this.findDomNodeHandler = this.findDomNodeHandler.bind(this);

    };

    findDomNodeHandler() {

        var myDiv = document.getElementById('myDiv');

        ReactDOM.findDOMNode(myDiv).style.color = 'green';

    }
```

```
render() {

    return (

        <div>

            <button onClick = {this.findDomNodeHandler}>FIND DOME NODE</button>

            <div id = "myDiv">NODE</div>

        </div>

    );

}

}

export default App;
```

The color of myDiv element changes to green, once the button is clicked.

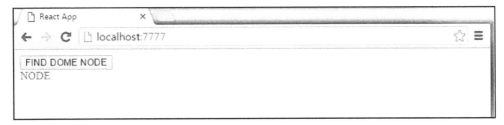

Note – Since the 0.14 update, most of the older component API methods are deprecated or removed to accommodate ES6.

Lifecycle Methods

- ComponentWillMount is executed before rendering, on both the server and the client side.

- ComponentDidMount is executed after the first render only on the client side. This is where AJAX requests and DOM or state updates should occur. This method is also used for integration with other JavaScript frameworks and any functions with delayed execution such as setTimeout or setInterval. We are using it to update the state so we can trigger the other lifecycle methods.

- ComponentWillReceiveProps is invoked as soon as the props are updated before another render is called. We triggered it from setNewNumber when we updated the state.

- ShouldComponentUpdate should return true or false value. This will determine if the component will be updated or not. This is set to true by default. If you are sure that the component doesn't need to render after state or props are updated, you can return false value.

- ComponentWillUpdate is called just before rendering.

- ComponentDidUpdate is called just after rendering.

- ComponentWillUnmount is called after the component is unmounted from the dom. We are unmounting our component in main.js.

In the following example, we will set the initial state in the constructor function. The setNewnumber is used to update the state. All the lifecycle methods are inside the Content component.

App.jsx

```
import React from 'react';


class App extends React.Component {
   constructor(props) {
      super(props);

      this.state = {
         data: 0
      }
      this.setNewNumber = this.setNewNumber.bind(this)
   };
   setNewNumber() {
      this.setState({data: this.state.data + 1})
   }
   render() {
      return (
         <div>
            <button onClick = {this.setNewNumber}>INCREMENT</button>
            <Content myNumber = {this.state.data}></Content>
         </div>
      );
   }
}
class Content extends React.Component {
   componentWillMount() {
      console.log('Component WILL MOUNT!')
   }
```

```
componentDidMount() {

    console.log('Component DID MOUNT!')

}

componentWillReceiveProps(newProps) {

    console.log('Component WILL RECIEVE PROPS!')

}

shouldComponentUpdate(newProps, newState) {

    return true;

}

componentWillUpdate(nextProps, nextState) {

    console.log('Component WILL UPDATE!');

}

componentDidUpdate(prevProps, prevState) {

    console.log('Component DID UPDATE!')

}

componentWillUnmount() {

    console.log('Component WILL UNMOUNT!')

}

render() {

    return (

        <div>

            <h3>{this.props.myNumber}</h3>

        </div>

    );

}

}

export default App;
```

Main.JS

```
import React from 'react';

import ReactDOM from 'react-dom';
```

```
import App from './App.jsx';

ReactDOM.render(<App/>, document.getElementById('app'));

setTimeout(() => {
   ReactDOM.unmountComponentAtNode(document.getElementById('app'));}, 10000);
```

After the initial render, we will get the following screen.

Features of ReactJS

JSX

In React, instead of using regular JavaScript for templating, it uses JSX. JSX is simple JavaScript which allows HTML quoting and uses these HTML tag syntax to render subcomponents. HTML syntax is processed into JavaScript calls of React Framework. We can also write in pure old JavaScript.

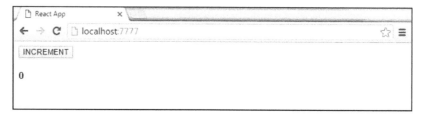

React Native

React has native libraries which were announced by Facebook in 2015, which provides the react architecture to native applications like IOS, Android and UPD.

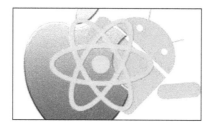

Single-way Data Flow

In React, a set of immutable values are passed to the components renderer as properties in its

HTML tags. Component cannot directly modify any properties but can pass a call back function with help of which we can do modifications. This complete process is known as "properties flow down; actions flow up".

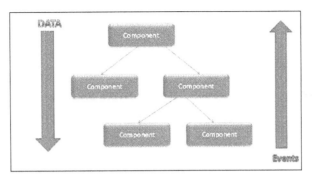

Virtual Document Object Model

React creates an in-memory data structure cache which computes the changes made and then updates the browser. This allows a special feature which enable programmer to code as if whole page is render on each change whereas react library only render components which actually change.

MeteorJS

MeteorJS is defining as the framework of Javascript that facilitates the application design in a very short period of time. MeteorJS is helped in the full-stack development of web or mobile application development. It works very fine with Mongo DB. Though it is also possible to integrate it with other databases by default, the database is Mongo DB.

- Meteors could be defined as the technology that provides a full-stack platform for creating web applications. It works best with the server and client in order to achieve it's a feature of providing a full-stack environment. In order to implement the MeteorJS, we have to use HTML, CSS, Mongo DB, and inbuilt JS functions. Before we begin work with this, we have to make the system ready for it.

- In MeteorJS, the application gets better connectivity with the backend and hence it could be considered as the web designing technology that works in frontend and backend as well. It can also be explained as the upgraded version of Javascript. On one hand, where Javascript is the client-side scripting language, on the other hand, MeteoJS works on both client and server-side.

- A server is required to work with MeteorJS so your system must be capable of it which could be done by installing MeteorJS in your machine. You can download and install the MeteorJS from their official website and then you will need to run the .meteor file using the command prompt in order to start of the service so that you can actually work with MeteorJS.

Working with MeteorJS

- Once the meteor is downloaded and installed. We have to run the .meteor file from where it is located which could be done following the code written in the below snap.

- We have to wait for the database and proxy is being started. Once you are all set to begin, now it turns to write your code and start implementing Meteor JS. Below is the HTML code that later has to be integrated with the JS file to being it's functionality to the webpage.

- After the HTML page now it turns to use the inbuilt functions of Javascript so that we can implement the MeteorJS. In the below image we will be defining what functionality we actually expecting from "hello". The statements defined in the below file will get integrated with the HTML page in order to design the webpage which will be the outcome of this.

- Once you are done with writing the code, now it turns to open the localhost and check the output. Based on the functionality that you have defined, it will perform. Below will be the outcome of these codes.

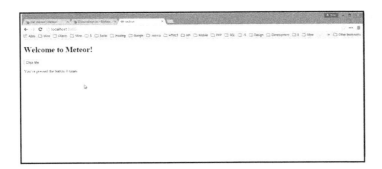

Features of Meteor JS

- With Meteor you can develop apps in JavaScript for a web browser, application server, and mobile environment.

- Meteor has several built-in features like hot code reload, automatic CSS & JS minification, and reactive templates.

- The app is created using JavaScript so you can use the same code on both client and server side.

- Meteor JS allows to develop and deploy Android and iOS apps through Cordova PhoneGap alliance.

- It provides helpful client-side technologies such as helpers, events, and templates.

- You can transform a web application into a smartphone app using Cordova with Meteor.

- It performs the updates automatically when any changes created in data of a database.

- It allows direct access to the database so you don't need to load the data from rest.

- It has efficient cloud platform 'Galaxy' which is very useful to deploy and monitor client applications.

- The dependency on a server for to update the app is ended as it instantly updates without interrupting the app users.

Advantages of MeteorJS

The reason for bringing MeteorJS was to introduce or highlight advantages in Javascript. It provides us some of the very important features and really endorsed by web application developers. Below are some of its common benefits.

- Full Stack development – MeteorJS introduces the functionality of full stack application development that enables developers to take leverage of the inbuilt classes in order to create an efficient application.

- Database integration – The application developed in the MeteorJS could be integrated with the database and the default database is Mongo DB. One can also replace the DB with whatever they are comfortable.

- Consumes less time – The very important part of using MeteorJS is, it makes the work gets completed in less time span due to the inbuilt functionality that could be used without being defined.

- Security – It is very exciting to know that the web or mobile application developed using it is ample secure and could be deployed without considering security as a primary concern.

jQuery

jQuery is a fast, small and feature-rich JavaScript library included in a single .js file.

jQuery makes a web developer's life easy. It provides many built-in functions using which you can accomplish various tasks easily and quickly.

The jQuery Important Features

- DOM Selection: jQuery provides Selectors to retrieve DOM element based on different criteria like tag name, id, css class name, attribute name, value, nth child in hierarchy etc.

- DOM Manipulation: You can manipulate DOM elements using various built-in jQuery functions. For example, adding or removing elements, modifying html content, css class etc.

- Special Effects: You can apply special effects to DOM elements like show or hide elements, fade-in or fade-out of visibility, sliding effect, animation etc.

- Events: jQuery library includes functions which are equivalent to DOM events like click, dblclick, mouseenter, mouseleave, blur, keyup, keydown etc. These functions automatically handle cross-browser issues.

- Ajax: jQuery also includes easy to use AJAX functions to load data from servers without reloading whole page.

- Cross-browser support: jQuery library automatically handles cross-browser issues, so the user does not have to worry about it. jQuery supports IE 6.0+, FF 2.0+, Safari 3.0+, Chrome and Opera 9.0+.

Advantages of JQuery

- Easy to learn: jQuery is easy to learn because it supports same JavaScript style coding.

- Write less do more: jQuery provides a rich set of features that increase developers' productivity by writing less and readable code.

- Excellent API Documentation: jQuery provides excellent online API documentation.

- Cross-browser support: jQuery provides excellent cross-browser support without writing extra code.

- Unobtrusive: jQuery is unobtrusive which allows separation of concerns by separating html and jQuery code.

The JQuery Selectors

The jQuery selector enables you to find DOM elements in your web page. Most of the times you will start with selector function $() in the jQuery.

Syntax

$(*selector expression, context*)

jQuery(*selector expression, context*)

- The selector expression parameter specifies a pattern to match the elements. The jQuery uses CSS selector patterns as well as its own pattern to match the elements.

- The context parameter is optional. It specifies elements in a DOM hierarchy from where jQuery starts searching for matching elements.

Let's see commonly used selectors in jQuery.

Select Elements by Name

The most common selector pattern is element name. Specifing an element name as string e.g. $('p') will return an array of all the <p> elements in a webpage.

The following figure shows which DOM elements will be returned from $('p') & $'(div').

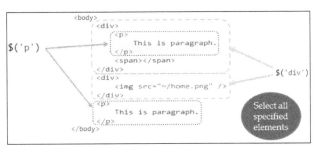

The jQuery Selectors Demo

As you can see in the above figure, $('div') will return all the <div> elements including its child elements.

Example: Select elements by name.

```
$('p').append('This is paragraph.'); // appends text to all p elements

$('div').append('This is div.); // appends text to all div elements

<div>

    <p></p>

    <p></p>

</div>

<p></p>

<div></div>
```

Select Elements by Id

You can get a particular element by using id selector pattern. Specify an id of an element for which you want to get the reference, starting with # symbol.

The following figure shows which DOM elements will be returned from $('#myDiv1') & $'(#prg2').

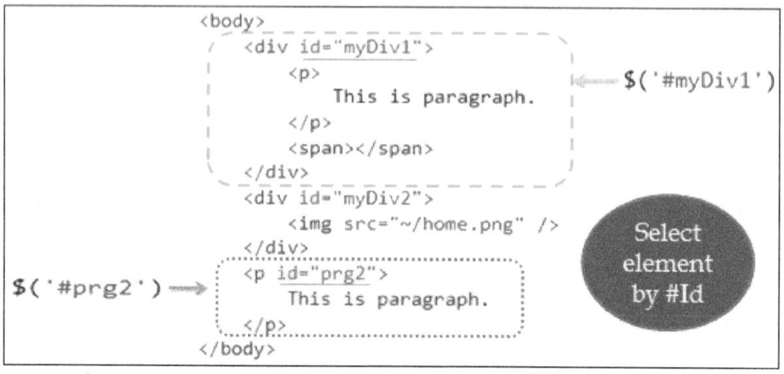

jQuery Id Selector Demo

Example: Select Element by #Id.

```
$('#impPrg').append('This element\'s id is "impPrg"');
```

```
$('#myDiv2').append('This element\'s id is "myDiv2"');
```

```
<div id="myDiv1">

    <p></p>

</div>
```

```
<p id="impPrg"></p>
```

```
<div id="myDiv2">

</div>
```

Select Elements by Attribute

jQuery also allows you to find an element based on attributes set on it. Specifing an attribute name in square brackets in $ function e.g. $('[class]') will return all the elements that have class attribute irrespective of value.

In the following example, jQuery returns all the elements that have class or contenteditable attribute irrespective of any value.

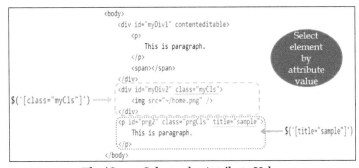

The jQuery Attribute Selector

Example: Select Elements by Attribute.

```
$('[class]').append('This element has class attribute');
```

```
<div id="myDiv1">

    <p></p>

</div>
```

```
<p id="impPrg" class="boldPrg"></p>
```

```
<div id="myDiv2" class="yellowDiv">

</div>
```

You can also specify a specific value of an attribute in attribute selector. For example, $('[class="-myCls"]') will return all the elements which have class attribute with myCls as a value.

The jQuery Selector by Attribute Value

Example: Select Element by Attribute Value.

```
$('[class="yellowDiv"]').append('This element includes class="yellowDiv" attri-
bute');
```

```
<div id="myDiv1">
```

```
    <p></p>

</div>


<p id="impPrg" class="boldPrg">This is paragraph.</p>


<div id="myDiv2" class="yellowDiv">

</div>
```

jQuery Selector Patterns

jQuery provides number of ways to select a specific DOM element(s). The following table lists the most important selector patterns.

Category	Selector	Description
Find by Element	$('p')	Find all <p> elements.
	$('p, div, code')	Find <p>,<div> and <code> elements.
Find Descendant Elements	$('div p')	Find all <p> elements which are descendants of <div>.
	$('div > p')	Find <p> which is child of <div>.
	$(*)	Find all elements.
Find by Id	$('#myDiv')	Find element whose id is *myDiv*.
	$('p#myPrg')	Find <p> element whose Id is *myPrg*.
	$('#myDiv1, #myDiv2')	Find multiple elements by id separated by comma.
Find by CSS Class	$('.myCSSClass')	Find all the elements with *class=myCSSClass*.
	$('.myCSSClass1, .myCSSClass2 ')	Finds all elements whose class attribute is set to *myCSSClass1* or *myCSSClass2*.
	$('div.myCSSClass')	Finds all <div> elements with *class=myCSSClass*.
	$('p:first-child')	Find all <p> elements, which is the first child of its parent element. (parent element can be anything)
Find by Attributes	$('[class]')	Find all the elements with the *class* attribute (whatever the value).
	$('div[class]')	Find all the <div> elements that have a *class* attribute (whatever the value).
Find by containing value of attribute	$('div[class=myCls]')	Find all the <div> elements whose class attributes are equal to *myCls*.
	$('div[class|=myCls]')	Find all the <div> elements whose class attributes are either equal to *myCls* or starting with *myCls* string followed by a hyphen (-).
	$('div[class *="myCls"]')	Selects <div> elements whose class attributes contain *myCls*.
	$('div[class~=myCls]')	Selects div elements whose class attributes contain *myCls*, delimited by spaces.

	$('div[class$=myCls]')$	Selects <div> elements whose class attributes value ends with *myCls*. The comparison is case sensitive.
	$('div[class!=myCls]')$	Selects <div> elements which does not have *class* attribute or value does not equal to myCls.
	$('div[class^=myCls]')$	Selects <div> elements whose *class* attribute value starts with myCls.
	$('div:contains("tutorialsteacher")'$	Find all <div> elements that contains the text *'tutorialsteacher'*.
Find by Input type	$(":button")$	Find all input whose type is button.
	$(':input[type="radio"]')$	Find all radio input types.
Even-Odd rows	$('tr:odd')$	Find all odd rows. (1,3,5,7)
	$('tr:even')$	Find all even rows.(0,2,4,6)

The jQuery Methods

The jQuery selector finds particular DOM element(s) and wraps them with jQuery object. For example, document.getElementById() in the JavaScript will return DOM object whereas $('#id') will return jQuery object. The following figure illustrates the difference.

```
<html>
<body>
    <div id="myDiv"></div>
</body>
</html>
```

document.getElementById('myDiv'); ──▶ Returns DOM Element: <div id="myDiv"></div>

$('#myDiv'); ───▶ Returns jQuery object: jQuery object
                                          <div id="myDiv"></div>

The jQuery Methods

As you can see in the above figure, document.getElementById function returns div element whereas jQuery selector returns jQuery object which is a wrapper around div element. So now, you can call jQuery methods of jQuery object which is returned by jQuery selector.

The jQuery provides various methods for different tasks e.g. manipulate DOM, events, ajax etc. The following table lists different categories of methods.

Category	Description	Imp Methods
DOM Manipulation	These methods manipulate DOM elements in some manner e.g. changing attribute, style attribute, adding and removing elements etc.	after(), append(), attr(), before(), more.
Traversing	These methods help in navigating from DOM element to another element in a parent child hierarchy e.g. finding ancestors, descendants or sibling element of a specified element.	children(), closest(), each(), first(), next(), filter(), parent(), siblings(), more.
CSS	These methods get and set css related properties of elements.	addClass(), css(), hasClass(), removeClass(), toggleClass() more.
Attributes	These methods get and set DOM attributes of elements.	attr(), html(), removeAttr(), prop(), val(), more.

Events	These methods are used to handle DOM or JavaScript events.	bind(), blur(), change(), click(), dblclick(), focus(), keyup(), key-down(), more.
Effects	These methods are used to add animation to elements.	animate(), fadeIn(), fadeOut(), hide(), show(), stop(), more.
Dimensions	These methods are used to get and set the CSS dimensions for the various properties.	height(), width(), inner-Height(), innerWidth(), more.
Forms	These methods and event handlers handle forms and their various elements.	blur(), change(), val(), submit(), more.
Ajax	These methods allow Ajax functionalities with jQuery e.g.	get(), getJson(), post(), load(), more.
Core	These methods are core methods in jQuery API.	jQuery(), holdReady(), when(), more.
Data	These methods allow us to associate arbitrary data with specific DOM elements.	data(), removeData(), queue(), dequeue(), clearQueue(), more.
Miscellaneous	These methods are useful in various tasks e.g. traversing elements, converting to array etc.	each(), index(), get(), toArray(), more.
Utilities	Utility methods are helpful in getting information on various things e.g. browser, function, array, window etc.	inArray(), isArray(), isFunction(), isNu-meric(), isWindow(), isXmlDoc(), more.

The following example shows how to use some of the jQuery methods to manipulate DOM elements.

Example: jQuery Methods

```
<!DOCTYPE html>


<html>

<head>

    <meta name="viewport" content="width=device-width" />

    <title>Index</title>

    <script type="text/javascript" src="~/Scripts/jquery-3.3.1.js"></script>

    <script type="">

        $(document).ready(function () {


            $('p').wrap('<div class="myCls">'); @* wrap all p with div *@

            $('#myDiv').hide(); @* hides div whose id is myDiv  *@
```

```
        $('span').attr(  @*sets style and width attribute on all span *@

            {

                'style': 'border:solid',

                'width': '100%'

            });

        $('p').append('This is p.'); @* append text to <p> *@


            $('span').before('<p>This is another p</p>'); @* insert <p> before
span  *@


        });

    </script>

</head>


<body>

    <div id="myDiv"></div>

    <p></p>

    <span></span>

</body>

</html>
```

DOM Manipulation Methods in jQuery

The jQuery provides various methods to add, edit or delete DOM element(s) in the HTML page.

The following table lists some important methods to add/remove new DOM elements.

Method	Description
append()	Inserts content to the end of element(s) which is specified by a selector.
before()	Inserts content (new or existing DOM elements) before an element(s) which is specified by a selector.
after()	Inserts content (new or existing DOM elements) after an element(s) which is specified by a selector.
prepend()	Insert content at the beginning of an element(s) specified by a selector.
remove()	Removes element(s) from DOM which is specified by selector.
replaceAll()	Replace target element(s) with specified element.
wrap()	Wrap an HTML structure around each element which is specified by selector.

The following figure shows how the DOM manipulation methods add new elements.

DOM Manipulation Methods

Let's have a quick overview of important DOM manipulation methods.

The JQuery after() Method

The jQuery after() method inserts content (new or existing DOM elements) after target element(s) which is specified by a selector.

Syntax

```
$('selector expression').after('content');
```

First of all, specify a selector to get the reference of target element(s) after which you want to add the content and then call after() method. Pass the content string as a parameter. Content string can be any valid HTML element.

Example: The jQuery after() Method.

```
$('#div1').after('<div style="background-color:yellow"> New div </div>');


<div id="div1">div 1

</div>


<div id="div2">div 2

</div>
```

Result:

```
<div id="div1">div 1

</div>


<div style="background-color:yellow"> New div </div>


<div id="div2">div 2

</div>
```

The jQuery before() Method

The jQuery before() method inserts content (new or existing DOM elements) before target element(s) which is specified by a selector.

Syntax

```
$('selector expression').before('content');
```

Specify a selector to get the reference of target element(s) before which you want to add the content and then call before() method. Pass the content string that can be any valid HTML element as parameter.

Example: jQuery before() Method.

```
$('#div1').before('<div style="background-color:yellow"> New div </div>');


<div id="div1">div 1

</div>


<div id="div2">div 2

</div>
```

Result:

```
<div style="background-color:yellow"> New div </div>

<div id="div1">div 1

</div>


<div id="div2">div 2

</div>
```

The JQuery Append() Method

The jQuery append() method inserts content to the end of target element(s) which is specified by a selector.

Syntax

```
$('selector expression').append('content');
```

First specify a selector expression to get the reference of an element(s) to which you want to append content, then call append() method and pass content string as a parameter.

Example: The jQuery append() Method.

```
$('p').append('World!');
```

```
<p>Hello </p>
```

Result:

```
<p>Hello World!</p>
```

The jQuery Prepend() Method

The jQuery prepend() method inserts content at the beginning of an element(s) specified by a selector.

Syntax

```
$('selector expression').prepend('content');
```

First specify a selector expression to get the reference of an element(s) to which you want to prepend the content, then call prepend() method and pass content string as a parameter.

Example: jQuery prepend() Method.

```
$('div').prepend('<p>This is prepended paragraph</p>');
```

```
<div>
            <label>This is div.</label>
</div>
```

```
Result:
```

```
<div>
            <p>This is prepended paragraph</p>
            <label>This is div.</label>
</div>
```

The jQuery Remove() Method

The jQuery remove() method removes element(s) as specified by a selector.

Syntax

```
$('selector expression').remove();
```

First specify a selector expression to get the reference of an element(s) which you want to remove from the document and then call remove() method.

Example: jQuery remove() Method.

```
$('label').remove();
```

```
<div>This is div.
                <label>This is label.</label>
</div>
```

Result:

```
<div>
    This is div.
</div>
```

The jQuery ReplaceAll() Method

The jQuery replaceAll() method replaces all target elements with specified element(s).

Syntax

```
$('content string').replaceAll('selector expression');
```

Here, syntax is different. First specify a content string as replacement element(s) and then call replaceAll() method with selector expression to specify a target element(s).

Example: jQuery replaceAll() Method.

```
$('<span>This is span</span>').replaceAll('p');
```

```
<div>
    <p>This is paragraph.</p>
</div>
```

```
<p>This is another paragraph.</p>
```

Result:

```
<div>
    <span>This is span</span>
</div>
<span>This is span</span>
```

The jQuery Wrap() Method

The jQuery wrap() method wrap each target element with specified content element.

Syntax

```
$('selector expression').wrap('content string');
```

Specify a selector to get target elements and then call wrap method and pass content string to wrap the target element(s).

Example: The jQuery wrap() Method.

```
$('span').wrap('<p></p>');
```

```
<div>

    <span>This is span.</span>

</div>

<span>This is span.</span>
```

Result:

```
<div>

    <p> <span>This is span.</span></p>

</div>

<p><span>This is span.</span></p>
```

Attributes Manipulation using jQuery

The following table lists jQuery methods to get or set value of attribute, property, text or html.

jQuery Method	Description
attr()	Get or set the value of specified attribute of the target element(s).
prop()	Get or set the value of specified property of the target element(s).
html()	Get or set html content to the specified target element(s).
text()	Get or set text for the specified target element(s).
val()	Get or set value property of the specified target element.

The following figure shows various jQuery methods to access DOM element's attributes, properties and values.

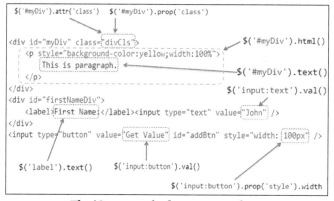

The jQuery methods to access values

Let's have a quick overview of important methods to access element's attributes.

The jQuery Attr() Method

The jQuery attr() method is used to get or set the value of specified attribute of DOM element.

Syntax

```
$('selector expression').attr('name','value');
```

First of all, specify a selector to get the reference of an element and call attr() method with attribute name parameter. To set the value of an attribute, pass value parameter along with name parameter.

Example: jQuery attr() Method.

```
$('p').attr('style'); // returns "font-size:16px;font-weight:bold"

$('div').attr('class','yellowDiv');  // adds class='divCls' to each div element


<div>

    This is div.

</div>

<p style="font-size:16px;font-weight:bold">

    This is paragraph.

</p>

<div>

    This is div.

</div>

<p>

    This is paragraph.

</p>
```

In the above example, $('p').attr('style') gets style attribute of first <p> element in a html page. It does not return style attributes of all the <p> elements.

The jQuery prop() Method

The jQuery prop() method gets or sets the value of specified property to the DOM element(s).

Syntax

```
$('selector expression').prop('name','value');
```

First of all, specify a selector to get the reference of an element(s) and call prop() method. Supply "name" parameter to get the value of that property. To set the value of a property, specify a value parameter along with name parameter.

Example: jQuery prop() Method.

```
var style = $('p').prop('style');

style.fontWeight; // returns "bold"


$('div').prop('class','yellowDiv'); // add class="yellowDiv" to all div elements


<div>

    This is div.

</div>
<p style="font-size:16px;font-weight:bold">

    This is paragraph.

</p>
<div>

    This is div.

</div>
<p>

    This is paragraph.

</p>
```

In the above example, $('p').prop('style') returns an object. You can get different style properties by using object.propertyName convention e.g. style.fontWeight. Do not include '-' as a property name.

The jQuery html() Method

The jQuery html() method gets or sets html content to the specified DOM element(s).

Syntax

```
$('selector expression').html('content');
```

First of all, specify a selector to get the reference of an element and call html() method without passing any parameter to get the inner html content. To set the html content, specify html content string as a parameter.

Example: jQuery html() Method.

```
$('#myDiv').html(); //returns innerHtml of #myDiv
```

```
//add <p>This is paragraph.</p> to #emptyDiv
$('#emptyDiv').html('<p>This is paragraph.</p>');


<div id="myDiv" class="yellowDiv">
    <p style="font-size:16px;font-weight:bold">
        This is paragraph.
    </p>
</div>
<div id="emptyDiv">
</div>
```

The jQuery Text() Method

The jQuery text() method gets or sets the text content to the specified DOM element(s).

Syntax

```
$('selector expression').text('content');
```

First of all, specify a selector to get the reference of an element and call text() method to get the textual content of an element. To set the text content, pass content string as a parameter.

Example: jQuery text() Method.

```
$('#myDiv').text(); //returns "This is paragraph."
$('p').text(); //returns "This is paragraph."


//removes all the content from #emptyDiv and inserts "This is some text." to it
$('#emptyDiv').text('This is some text.');


<div id="myDiv" class="divCls">
    <p style="font-size:16px;font-weight:bold">
        This is paragraph.
    </p>
</div>
<div id="emptyDiv">
</div>
```

Please note that text() method only returns text content inside the element and not the innerHtml.

The jQuery val() Method

The jQuery val() method gets or sets value property to the specified DOM element(s).

Syntax

```
$('selector expression').val('value');
```

First of all, specify a selector to get the reference of an element and call val() method to get the value of value property. To set the text content, pass content string as a parameter.

Example: jQuery val() Method.

```
$('input:Submit').val(); //returns "Save"


//set value of input text to "Steve"

$('input:text').val('Steve');


$('input:text').val(); //returns "Steve"


<div>

    <label>Name:</label><input type="text" />

</div>


<div>

    <input type="Submit" value="Save" />

</div>
```

In the above example, val() method returns value of "value" property. If element does not support value property then val() method returns null.

Manipulate DOM Element's Dimensions using jQuery

The jQuery library includes various methods to manipulate DOM element's dimensions like height, width, offset, position etc.

The following table lists all the jQuery methods to get or set DOM element's dimensions.

jQuery Method	Description
height()	Get or set height of the specified element(s).
innerHeight()	Get or set inner height (padding + element's height) of the specified element(s).
outerHeight()	Get or set outer height (border + padding + element's height) of the specified element(s).

offset()	Get or set left and top coordinates of the specified element(s).
position()	Get the current coordinates of the specified element(s).
width()	Get or set the width of the specified element(s).
innerWidth()	Get or set the inner width (padding + element's width) of the specified element(s).
outerWidth()	Get or set outer width (border + padding + element's width) of the specified element(s).

The following figure shows various dimensions of an element-

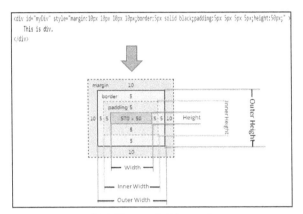

DOM Element's Dimensions

The jQuery Height() Method

The jQuery height()method gets or sets height of the specified DOM element(s).

Syntax

```
$('selector expression').height(value);
```

Specify a selector to get the reference of an element and call height() method to get the height in pixel. To set the height of specified elements, specify height as integer parameter in height() method.

Example: jQuery height() Method.

```
$('#myDiv').height(); //returns height of #myDiv in pixels

$('p').height(); //returns height in pixel


//set height of all div elements

$('div').height(100);


<div id="myDiv" >

    This is div.

</div>
```

```
<p>
    This is paragraph.
</p>
```

The jQuery Width() Method

The jQuery width() method gets or sets width of the specified DOM element(s).

Syntax

```
$('selector expression').width(value);
```

Specify a selector to get the reference of an element and call width() method to get the width in pixel. Specify width as integer parameter to set the width.

Example: jQuery width() Method.

```
$('#myDiv').width(); //returns width of #myDiv in pixels

$('p').width(); //returns width of p in pixel


//set width of all div elements
$('div').width(100);


<div id="myDiv" >
    This is div.
</div>


<p>
    This is paragraph.
</p>
```

The jQuery Offset() Method

The jQuery offset() method gets or sets coordinates of the specified element(s).

Syntax

```
$('selector expression').offset(options);
```

Specify a selector to get the reference of an element and call offset() method to get the jQuery object which has left and top property. Specify JSON object with left and top property with the coordinates where you want to move the element.

Example: jQuery offset() Method.

```
var ofs = $('#myDiv').offset();
```

```
alert('left:' + ofs.left + ', top: ' + ofs.top);


$('p').offset({ left:100, top:200});


<div id="myDiv" >

    This is div.

</div>


<p>

    This is paragraph.

</p>
```

Traversing DOM Elements using jQuery

The jQuery library includes various methods to traverse DOM elements in a DOM hierarchy.

The following table lists jQuery methods for traversing DOM elements.

jQuery Methods	Description
children()	Get all the child elements of the specified element(s).
each()	Iterate over specified elements and execute specified call back function for each element.
find()	Get all the specified child elements of each specified element(s).
first()	Get the first occurrence of the specified element.
next()	Get the immediately following sibling of the specified element.
parent()	Get the parent of the specified element(s).
prev()	Get the immediately preceding sibling of the specified element.
siblings()	Get the siblings of each specified element(s).

The following figure shows how the jQuery traversing methods get DOM elements.

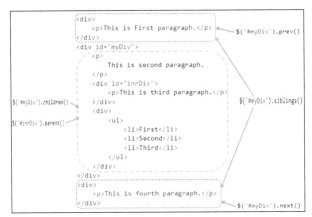

Traversing DOM Elements

Let's look at some of the important jQuery traversing methods.

The jQuery Each() Method

The jQuery each() method iterates over each specified element (specified using selector) and executes callback function for each element.

Syntax

```
$('selector expression').each(callback function);
```

To begin, specify a selector to get the reference of elements and call each() method with callback function, which will be executed for each element.

Example: jQuery each() method.

```
$('p').each(function (index) {
        alert('index' + index + ', text: ' + $(this).text());
    });
```

```
<div>
    <p>This is First paragraph.</p>
</div>
<div id="myDiv">
    <p>
        This is second paragraph.
    </p>
    <div id="inrDiv">
        <p>This is third paragraph.</p>
    </div>
    <div>
        <ul>
            <li>First</li>
            <li>Second</li>
            <li>Third</li>
        </ul>
    </div>
</div>
```

```
<div>
    <p>This is fourth paragraph.</p>
</div>
```

Result:

```
Index:0, text: This is first paragraph.

Index:1, text: This is second paragraph.

Index:2, text: This is third paragraph.

Index:3, text: This is fourth paragraph.
```

The jQuery Children() Method

The jQuery children() method get the child element of each element specified using selector expression.

Syntax

```
$('selector expression').children();
```

First, specify a selector to get the reference of an element(s) and call children() method to get all the child elements.

Example: jQuery children() method.

```
$('#myDiv').children().each(function (index) {
        alert('Index: ' + index + ', html: ' + $(this).html());
    });


<div>
    <p>This is First paragraph.</p>
</div>
<div id="myDiv">
    <p>
        This is second paragraph.
    </p>
    <div id="inrDiv">
        <p>This is third paragraph.</p>
    </div>
```

```
<div>
    <ul>
        <li>First</li>
        <li>Second</li>
        <li>Third</li>
    </ul>
</div>
</div>
<div>
    <p>This is fourth paragraph.</p>
</div>
```

Result:

```
Index:0, html: <p>
                   This is second paragraph.
               </p>
Index:1, html: <div id="inrDiv">
                   <p>This is third paragraph.</p>
               </div>
Index:2, html: <div>
                   <ul>
                       <li>First</li>
                       <li>Second</li>
                       <li>Third</li>
                   </ul>
               </div>
```

The jQuery Find() Method

The jQuery find() method returns all the matching child elements of specified element(s).

Syntax

```
$('selector expression').find('selector expression to find child elements');
```

Specify a selector to get the reference of an element(s) whose child elements you want to find and then call find() method with selector expression to get all the matching child elements. You can iterate child elements using each method.

Example: jQuery find() method.

```
$('#myDiv').find('p').each(function(index){
            alert('index' + index + ', text: ' + $(this).text());
    });


<div>
    <p>This is First paragraph.</p>
</div>
<div id="myDiv">
    <p>
        This is second paragraph.
    </p>
    <div id="inrDiv">
        <p>This is third paragraph.</p>
    </div>
    <div>
        <ul>
            <li>First</li>
            <li>Second</li>
            <li>Third</li>
        </ul>
    </div>
</div>
<div>
    <p>This is fourth paragraph.</p>
</div>
```

Result:

```
Index:0, text: This is second paragraph.
Index:1, text: This is third paragraph.
```

The jQuery Next() Method

The jQuery next() method gets the immediately following sibling of the specified element.

Syntax

```
$('selector expression').next();
```

Specify a selector to get the reference of an element of which you want to get next element and then call next() method.

Example: jQuery next() method.

```
alert('Next element to #myDiv: ' + $('#myDiv').next().html());


alert('Next element to #inrDiv: ' + $('#inrDiv').next().html());


<div>
    <p>This is First paragraph.</p>
</div>
<div id="myDiv">
    <p>
        This is second paragraph.
    </p>
    <div id="inrDiv">
        <p>This is third paragraph.</p>
    </div>
    <div>
        <ul>
            <li>First</li>
            <li>Second</li>
            <li>Third</li>
        </ul>
    </div>
</div>
<div>
    <p>This is fourth paragraph.</p>
</div>
```

Result:

```
Next element to #myDiv: <div>

                        <p>This is fourth paragraph.</p>

             </div>


Next element to #inrDiv: <ul>

                        <li>First</li>

                        <li>Second</li>

                        <li>Third</li>

             </ul>
```

The jQuery Parent() Method

The jQuery parent() method gets the immediate parent element of the specified element.

Syntax

```
$('selector expression').parent();
```

Specify a selector to get the reference of an element of which you want to get the parent element and then call parent() method.

Example: jQuery parent() method.

```
alert('Parent element of #inrDiv: ' + $('#inrDiv').parent().html());


<div>

    <p>This is First paragraph.</p>

</div>

<div id="myDiv">

    <p>

        This is second paragraph.

    </p>

    <div id="inrDiv">

        <p>This is third paragraph.</p>

    </div>
```

```
<div>
    <ul>
        <li>First</li>
        <li>Second</li>
        <li>Third</li>
    </ul>
</div>
</div>
<div>
    <p>This is fourth paragraph.</p>
</div>
```

Result:

```
Parent element of #inrDiv: <p>
                        This is second paragraph.
        </p>
        <div id="inrDiv">
            <p>This is third paragraph.</p>
        </div>
        <div>
            <ul>
                <li>First</li>
                <li>Second</li>
                <li>Third</li>
            </ul>
        </div>
```

The jQuery Siblings() Method

The jQuery siblings() method gets all siblings of the specified DOM element(s).

Syntax

```
$('selector expression').siblings();
```

Specify a selector to get the reference of an element of which you want to get the siblings and call siblings() method.

Tips: You can iterate sibling elements using each() method.

Example: jQuery siblings() method

```
$('#myDiv').siblings().css({"color": "green", "border": "2px solid green"});
```

```
<div>
    <p>This is First paragraph.</p>
</div>
<div id="myDiv">
    <p>
        This is myDiv.
</div>
<div>
    <p>This is second paragraph.</p>
</div>
```

CSS Manipulation using jQuery

The jQuery library includes various methods to manipulate style properties and CSS class of DOM element(s).

The following table lists jQuery methods for styling and css manipulation.

jQuery Methods	Description
css()	Get or set style properties to the specified element(s).
addClass()	Add one or more class to the specified element(s).
hasClass()	Determine whether any of the specified elements are assigned the given CSS class.
removeClass()	Remove a single class, multiple classes, or all classes from the specified element(s).
toggleClass()	Toggles between adding/removing classes to the specified elements.

The following figure shows how jQuery methods changes style and css class of the DOM elements.

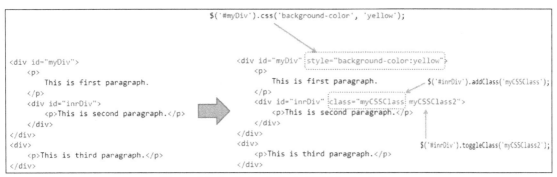

jQuery Methods for Style & CSS Manipulation

Let's have an overview of important jQuery methods for style and css manipulation.

The jQuery css() Method

The jQuery css() method gets or sets style properties to the specified element(s).

Syntax

```
$('selector expression').css('style property name','value');


$('selector expression').css({

                            'style property name':'value',

                });
```

Specify a selector to get the reference of an elements to which you want to set the style property and then call css() method with style property name and value parameter. You can also set multiple style properties by passing JSON object with 'style property name':'value'.

Example: jQuery css() Method.

```
$('#myDiv').css('background-color','yellow');
$('p').css({'background-color': 'red','width':'400px'});


$('#myDiv').css('background-color'); // returns rgb(255,255,0) for yellow color


<div id="myDiv">

    <p>This is first paragraph.</p>

</div>

<div>

    <p>This is second paragraph.</p>

</div>

<div >

    <p>This is third paragraph.</p>

</div>
```

In the above example, we set background-color of #myDiv and font styles to all <p> elements. The same way, we can get value of any style properties using css() method by specifying property name as first parameter.

The jQuery AddClass() method

The jQuery addClass() method adds single or multiple css class to the specified element(s).

Syntax

```
$('selector expression').addClass('css class name');
```

First specify a selector to get the reference of an elements to which you want to set the css property and then call addClass() method with one or multiple class names as a string parameter. Multiple class names must be separated by space.

Example: jQuery addClass() Method.

```
$('#myDiv').addClass('yellowDiv');
```

```
$('p').addClass('impPrg');
```

```
<div id="myDiv">

    <p>

        This is first paragraph.

    </p>

</div>

<div>

    <p>This is second paragraph.</p>

</div>

<div >

    <p>This is third paragraph.</p>

</div>
```

In the above example, we set css class of individual <div> element (#myDiv) as well as multiple <p> elements using addClass() method.

The jQuery ToggleClass() Method

The jQuery toggleClass() method toggles between adding/removing classes to the specified elements.

Syntax

```
$('selector expression').toggleClass('css class name');
```

Specify a selector to get the reference of an elements to which you want to toggle css classes and then call toggleClass() method with css class name as a string parameter.

Example: jQuery toggleClass() Method.

```
$('#myDiv').toggleClass('redDiv');
```

```
<div id="myDiv" class="yellowDiv">

</div>
```

In the above example, css class yellowDiv will be first added into div element and then removed. Thus, css class will be added or removed consecutively.

The jQuery Animation

jQuery includes methods which give special effects to the elements on hiding, showing, changing style properties, and fade-in or fade-out operation. These special effect methods can be useful in building an interactive user interface.

The following table lists jQuery methods for adding special effects to the DOM elements.

jQuery Methods for Special Effects	Description
animate()	Perform custom animation using element's style properties.
queue()	Show or manipulate the queue of functions to be executed on the specified element.
stop()	Stop currently running animations on the specified element(s).
fadeIn()	Display specified element(s) by fading them to opaque.
fadeOut()	Hides specified element(s) by fading them to transparent.
fadeTo()	Adjust the opacity of the specified element(s)
fadeToggle()	Display or hide the specified element(s) by animating their opacity.
hide()	Hide specified element(s).
show()	Display specified element(s).
toggle()	Display hidden element(s) or hide visible element(s).
slideUp()	Hide specified element(s) with sliding up motion.
slideDown()	Display specified element(s) with sliding down motion.
slideToggle()	Display or hide specified element(s) with sliding motion.

Let's look at some important methods for special effects.

The jQuery Animate() Method

The jQuery animate() method performs custom animation using element's style properties. The animate() method changes existing style properties to the specified properties with motion.

Specify a selector to get the reference of an element to which you want to add animation effect and then call animate() method with JSON object for style properties, speed of animation and other options.

Syntax

```
$('selector expression').animate({ stylePropertyName : 'value'},

                            duration,
```

```
                    easing,

                    callback);
```

```
$('selector expression').animate({ propertyName : 'value'},{ options });
```

Apply Animation

In the following example, we are changing height and width of the element with animation.

Example: jQuery animate() Method.

```
$('#myDiv').animate({
            height: '200px',
            width: '200px'
      });
```

```
<div id="myDiv" class="redDiv">
</div>
```

Set Animation Duration

You can apply animation duration in miliseconds as a second parameter of animate() method.

Example: Set Duration.

```
$('#myDiv').animate({
                  height: '200px',
                  width: '200px'
            },
            5000);
```

```
<div id="myDiv" class="redDiv">
</div>
```

Apply Easing Method

Specify a string parameter indicating which easing function to use for the transition. The jQuery library provides two easing function: linear and swing.

Example: Apply Easing Method.

```
$('#myDiv').animate({
```

```
                height: '200px',

                width: '200px'

        },

        5000, 'swing');
```

```
<div id="myDiv" class="redDiv">

</div>
```

Callback Function on Animation Complete

Specify a callback function to execute when animation is complete.

Example: Specify Callback Function.

```
$('#myDiv').animate({

                height: '200px',

                width: '200px'

        },

        5000,

        function () {

            $('#msgDiv').append('Animation completed');

        });

    });
```

```
<div id="myDiv" class="redDiv">

</div>
```

```
<div id="msgDiv"></div>
```

Specify Animation Options

You can specify various options as JSON object. The options include duration, easing, queue, step, progress, complete, start, done and always. Visit api.jquery.com for more information.

Example: Specify Options.

```
$('#myDiv').animate({

                height: '200px',
```

```
                    width: '200px'
            },
            {     // options parameter
            duration: 5000,
            complete: function () {
                $(this).animate({
                    height: '100px',
                    width: '100px'
                }, 5000,
                function () {
                    $('#msgDiv').text('Animation completed..');
                });
            },
            start: function () {
                $('#msgDiv').append('starting animation..');
            }
        });
```

```
<div id="msgDiv"></div>
```

```
<div id="myDiv" class="redDiv">
</div>
```

The jQuery Queue() Method

The jQuery queue() method shows or manipulates the queue of special effect functions to be executed on the specified element.

Syntax

```
$('selector expression').queue();
```

Example: jQuery queue() Method.

```
$('#myDiv').toggle(500);
```

```
$('#myDiv').fadeOut(500);
```

```
$('#myDiv').fadeIn(500);

$('#myDiv').slideDown(500);

$('#msgDiv').append('Animation functions: ' + $('#myDiv').queue().length);
```

```
<div id="msgDiv"></div>
```

```
<div id="myDiv" class="redDiv">
</div>
```

The jQuery FadeIn() Method

The jQuery fadeIn() method displays specified element(s) by fading them to opaque.

Syntax

```
$('selector expression').fadeIn(speed, easing, callback);
```

Example: jQuery fadeIn() Method.

```
$('#myDiv').fadeIn(5000, function () {
        $('#msgDiv').append('fadeIn() completed.')
    });
```

```
<div id="myDiv" class="redDiv">
</div>
```

```
<div id="msgDiv"></div>
```

The jQuery FadeOut() Method

The jQuery fadeOut() method hides specified element(s) by fading them to transparent.

Syntax

```
$('selector expression').fadeOut(speed, easing, callback);
```

Example: jQuery fadeOut() Method.

```
$('#div1').fadeOut(5000, function () {
        $('#msgDiv').append('fadeOut() completed.')
    });
```

```
<div id="msgDiv"></div>
```

```
<div id="myDiv" class="redDiv">
</div>
```

The jQuery hide() and show() Method

The jQuery hide() method hides and show() method displays the specified element. You can specify speed, easing and callback function which will be executed when hide/show completes.

Syntax

```
$('selector expression').hide(speed, easing, callback);

$('selector expression').show(speed, easing, callback);
```

Example: jQuery hide() & show() Methods.

```
$('#div1').hide(500, function () {
                $('#msgDiv').append('Red div is hidden.')
        });
```

```
$('#div2').hide(500, function () {
                $('#msgDiv').append('Yellow div is hidden.')
        });
```

```
<div id="div1" class="redDiv">
</div>
```

```
<div id="div2" class="yellowDiv">
</div>
```

The jQuery Toggle() Method

The jQuery toggle() method hides or displays specified element(s).

Syntax

```
$('selector expression').toggle(speed, easing, callback)
```

Example: jQuery toggle() Method.

```
$('#myDiv').toggle(500, function () {

        $('#msgDiv').append('fadeOut completed.')

    });



<div id="myDiv" class="redDiv">

</div>
```

The jQuery Events

In most web applications, the user does some action to perform an operation. For example, user clicks on save button to save the edited data in a web page. Here, clicking on the button is a user's action, which triggers click event and click event handler (function) saves data.

Event

The jQuery Event Methods

The jQuery library provides methods to handle DOM events. Most jQuery methods correspond to native DOM events.

The following table lists all jQuery methods and corresponding DOM events.

Category	jQuery Method	DOM Event
Form events	blur	onblur
	change	onchange
	focus	onfocus
	focusin	onfocusin
	select	onselect
	submit	onsubmit
Keyboard events	keydown	onkeydown
	keypress	onkeypress
	keyup	onkeyup
	focusout	
Mouse events	click	onclick
	dblclick	ondblclick
	focusout	

	hover	
	mousedown	onmousedown
	mouseenter	onmouseenter
	mouseleave	onmouseleave
	mousemove	onmousemove
	mouseout	onmouseout
	mouseover	onmouseover
	mouseup	onmouseup
	Toggle	
Browser events	Error	onerror()
	Resize	onresize
	Scroll	onscroll
Document loading	Load	onload
	Ready	
	Unload	onunload

Event Handling

To handle DOM events using jQuery methods, first get the reference of DOM element(s) using jQuery selector and invoke appropriate jQuery event method.

The following example shows how to handle button click event.

Example:Handle Button Click Event.

```
$('#saveBtn').click(function () {

    alert('Save button clicked');

});


<input type="button" value="Save" id="saveBtn" />
```

In the above example, we first use id selector to get a reference of 'Save' button and then call click method. We have specified handler function as a callback function, which will be called whenever click event of Save button is triggered.

Event Object

jQuery passes an event object to every event handler function. The event object includes important properties and methods for cross-browser consistency e.g. target, pageX, pageY, relatedTarget etc.

Example: jQuery Event Object.

```
$('#saveBtn').click(function (eventObj) {

    alert('X =' + eventObj.pageX + ', Y =' + eventObj.pageY);
```

```
});
```

```
<input type="button" value="Save" id="saveBtn" />
```

This Keyword in event handler.

This keyword in an event handler represents a DOM element which raised an event.

Example: This in event handler.

```
$(':button').click(function (eventObj) {
    alert(this.value + ' ' + this.type + ' clicked');
});
```

```
<input type="button" value="Save" id="saveBtn" />
<input type="button" value="Delete" id="delBtn" />
<input type="button" value="Clear" id="clearBtn" />
```

Hover Events

jQuery provides various methods for mouse hover events e.g. mouseenter, mouseleave, mousemove, mouseover, mouseout and mouseup.

Example: Hover Events.

```
$('#myDiv').mouseenter(function (data) {
        $(this).css('background-color','green');
    });
```

```
$('#myDiv').mouseleave(function (data) {
        $(this).css('background-color','red');
    });
```

```
<div id="myDiv" style="width:100px;height:100px">
</div>
```

You can use hover() method instead of handling mouseenter and mouseleave events separately.

Example: hover() Method.

```
$('#myDiv').hover(function () {
```

```
    $(this).css('background-color','green');

},

function () {

    $(this).css('background-color','red');

});
```

```
<div id="myDiv" style="width:100px;height:100px">

</div>
```

Event Binding using on():

The jQuery allows you to attach an event handler for one or more events to the selected elements using on method.

Internally all of the shorthand methods uses on() method. The on() method gives you more flexibility in event binding.

Syntax

```
on(types, selector, data, fn )
```

- Types = One or more space-separated event types and optional namespaces.
- Selector = selector string.
- Data = data to be passed to the handler in event.data when an event is triggered.
- Fn = A function to execute when the event is triggered.

Example: Event Binding using on.

```
$('#saveBtn').on('click',function () {

    alert('Save Button clicked');

});
```

```
<input type="button" value="Save" id="saveBtn" />
```

You can use selector to filter the descendants of the selected elements that trigger the event.

Example: Event Binding using on.

```
$('#myDiv').on('click',':button', function () {

    alert('Button clicked');

});
```

```
<div id="myDiv" >

    <input type="button" value="Save" id="saveBtn" />


    <input type="button" value="Add" id="addBtn" />
</div>


<input type="button" value="Delete" id="delBtn" />
```

In the above example, we specify ':button' selector. So click event triggered by buttons in <div> tag whose id is myDiv, will only be handled.

Binding Multiple Events

You can also specify multiple event types separated by space.

Example: Multiple Events Binding.

```
$( 'myDiv' ).on('mouseenter mouseleave', function() {
    $(this).text('The mouse entered or left from the div' );
});


<div id="myDiv" style="width:100px;height:100px">
</div>
```

Specify Named Function as Event Handler

You can create separate functions and specify that as a handler. This is useful if you want to use the same handler for different events or events on different elements.

Example: Binding Named Function to Event.

```
var mouseHandler = function() {
    alert( "The mouse entered" );
};


$('#myDiv').on('mouseenter', mouseHandler);


<div id="myDiv" style="width:100px;height:100px">
</div>
```

jQuery on() method is replacement of live() and delegate() method.

Event Bubbling

The following example demonstrates event bubbling in jQuery.

Example: Event Bubbling.

```
$('div').click(function (event) {
    alert( event.target.tagName + ' clicked');
});


<div>
    <p>
        <span>This is span.</span>
    </p>
</div>
```

The jQuery Ajax Introduction

Ajax stands for "Asynchronous JavaScript and XML".

JavaScript includes features of sending asynchronous http request using XMLHttpRequest object. Ajax is about using this ability of JavaScript to send asynchronous http request and get the xml data as a response (also in other formats) and update the part of a web page (using JavaScript) without reloading or refreshing entire web page.

The following figure illustrates the Ajax functionality-

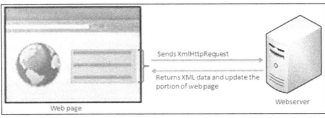

Ajax

The jQuery library includes various methods to send Ajax requests. These methods internally use XMLHttpRequest object of JavaScript. The following table lists all the Ajax methods of jQuery.

jQuery Ajax Methods	Description
ajax()	Sends asynchronous http request to the server.
get()	Sends http GET request to load the data from the server.
Post()	Sends http POST request to submit or load the data to the server.
getJSON()	Sends http GET request to load JSON encoded data from the server.
getScript()	Sends http GET request to load the JavaScript file from the server and then executes it.
load()	Sends http request to load the html or text content from the server and add them to DOM element(s).

The jQuery library also includes following events which will be fired based on the state of the Ajax request.

jQuery Ajax Events	Description
ajaxComplete()	Register a handler function to be called when Ajax requests complete.
ajaxError()	Register a handler function to be called when Ajax requests complete with an error.
ajaxSend()	Register a handler function to be called before Ajax request is sent.
ajaxStart()	Register a handler function to be called when the first Ajax request begins.
ajaxStop()	Register a handler function to be called when all the Ajax requests have completed.
ajaxSuccess()	Register a handler function to be called when Ajax request completes successfully.

Advantages of jQuery Ajax

- Cross-browser support,

- Simple methods to use,

- Ability to send GET and POST requests,

- Ability to Load JSON, XML, HTML or Scripts.

The jQuery Ajax() Method

The jQuery ajax() method provides core functionality of Ajax in jQuery. It sends asynchronous HTTP requests to the server.

Syntax

```
$.ajax(url);
```

```
$.ajax(url,[options]);
```

Parameter description:

- URL: A string URL to which you want to submit or retrieve the data.

- Options: Configuration options for Ajax request. An options parameter can be specified using JSON format. This parameter is optional.

The following table list all the options available for configuring Ajax request.

Options	Description
accepts	The content type sent in the request header that tells the server what kind of response it will accept in return.
async	By default, all requests are sent asynchronously. Set it false to make it synchronous.
beforeSend	A callback function to be executed before Ajax request is sent.
cache	A boolean indicating browser cache. Default is true.
complete	A callback function to be executed when request finishes.
contentType	A string containing a type of content when sending MIME content to the server. Default is "application/x-www-form-urlencoded; charset=UTF-8".

crossDomain	A boolean value indicating whether a request is a cross-domain.
data	A data to be sent to the server. It can be JSON object, string or array.
dataType	The type of data that you're expecting back from the server.
error	A callback function to be executed when the request fails.
global	A Boolean indicating whether to trigger a global Ajax request handler or not. Default is true.
headers	An object of additional header key/value pairs to send along with request.
ifModified	Allow the request to be successful only if the response has changed since the last request. This is done by checking the Last-Modified header. Default value is false.
isLocal	Allow the current environment to be recognized as local.
jsonp	Override the callback function name in a JSONP request. This value will be used instead of 'callback' in the 'callback=?' part of the query string in the url.
jsonpCallback	String containing the callback function name for a JSONP request.
mimeType	String containing a mime type to override the XMLHttpRequest mime type.
password	A password to be used with XMLHttpRequest in response to an HTTP access authentication request.
processData	A Boolean indicating whether data assigned to data option will be converted to a query string. Default is true.
statusCode	A JSON object containing numeric HTTP codes and functions to be called when the response has the corresponding code.
success	A callback function to be executed when Ajax request succeeds.
timeout	A number value in milliseconds for the request timeout.
type	A type of http request e.g. POST, PUT and GET. Default is GET.
url	A string containing the URL to which the request is sent.
username	A username to be used with XMLHttpRequest in response to an HTTP access authentication request.
xhr	A callback for creating the XMLHttpRequest object.
xhrFields	An object of fieldName-fieldValue pairs to set on the native XMLHttpRequest object.

Let's see how to send http requests using $.ajax() (or jQuery.ajax()) method.

Send Ajax Request

The ajax() methods performs asynchronous http request and gets the data from the server. The following example shows how to send a simple Ajax request.

Example: jQuery Ajax Request.

```
$.ajax('/jquery/getdata',   // request url
    {
        success: function (data, status, xhr) {// success callback function
            $('p').append(data);
        }
});


<p></p>
```

In the above example, first parameter '/getData' of ajax() method is a url from which we want to retrieve the data.

The second parameter is options parameter in JSON format where we have specified callback function that will be executed when request succeeds. You can configure other options as mentioned in the above table.

The following example shows how to get the JSON data using ajax() method.

Example: Get JSON Data.

```
$.ajax('/jquery/getjsondata',

{

    dataType: 'json', // type of response data

    timeout: 500,     // timeout milliseconds

    success: function (data,status,xhr) {    // success callback function

        $('p').append(data.firstName + ' ' + data.middleName + ' ' + data.last-
Name);

    },

    error: function (jqXhr, textStatus, errorMessage) { // error callback

        $('p').append('Error: ' + errorMessage);

    }

});


<p></p>
```

In the above example, first parameter is a request url which will return JSON data. In the options parameter, we have specified dataType and timeout options. The dataType option specifies the type of response data, in this case it is JSON. The timeout parameter specifies request timeout in milliseconds. We have also specified callback functions for error and success.

The ajax() method returns an object of jQuery XMLHttpRequest. The following example shows how to use jQuery XMLHttpRequest object.

Example: ajax() Method.

```
var ajaxReq = $.ajax('GetJsonData', {

                        dataType: 'json',

                        timeout: 500

            });
```

```
ajaxReq.success(function (data, status, jqXhr) {

    $('p').append(data.firstName + ' ' + data.middleName + ' ' + data.last-
Name);

    })


    ajaxReq.error(function (jqXhr, textStatus, errorMessage) {

        $('p').append('Error: ' + errorMessage);

    })
```

`<p></p>`

Send http POST Request using Ajax()

The ajax() method can send all type of http requests. The following example sends http POST request to the server.

Example: Send POST Request.

```
$.ajax('/jquery/submitData', {
    type: 'POST',  // http method
    data: { myData: 'This is my data.' },  // data to submit
    success: function (data, status, xhr) {
        $('p').append('status: ' + status + ', data: ' + data);
    },
    error: function (jqXhr, textStatus, errorMessage) {
            $('p').append('Error' + errorMessage);
    }
});
```
`<p></p>`

The jQuery get() Method

The jQuery get() method sends asynchronous http GET request to the server and retrieves the data.

Syntax

```
$.get(url, [data],[callback]);
```

Parameters Description:

- URL: request URL from which you want to retrieve the data.

- Data: data to be sent to the server with the request as a query string.

- Callback: function to be executed when request succeeds.

The following example shows how to retrieve data from a text file.

Example: jQuery get() Method.

```
$.get('/data.txt',  // url

        function (data, textStatus, jqXHR) {  // success callback

            alert('status: ' + textStatus + ', data:' + data);

    });
```

In the above example, first parameter is a url from which we want to retrieve the data. Here, we want to retrieve data from a txt file located at mydomain.com/data.txt. Please note that you don't need to give base address.

The second parameter is a callback function that will be executed when this GET request succeeds. This callback function includes three parameters data, textStatus and jQuery wrapper of XML-HttpRequest object. Data contains response data, textStatus contains status of request and jqXHR is a jQuery XMLHttpRequest object which you can use for further process.

The following example shows how to retrieve JSON data using get() method.

Example: Retrieve JSON Data using get().

```
$.get('/jquery/getjsondata', {name:'Steve'}, function (data, textStatus, jqXHR)
{

    $('p').append(data.firstName);

});


<p></p>
```

In the above example, first parameter is a url from which we want to retrieve JSON data. This url can be a web service or any other url that returns data in JSON format.

The second parameter is data to be sent to the server as a query string. We have specified name parameter with value 'Steve' in the JSON format. So now, the request url would look like http://mydomain.com/jquery/getjsondata?name=Steve

The third parameter is a callback function that will be executed when this GET request succeeds.

The jQuery GetJSON() Method

The jQuery getJSON() method sends asynchronous http GET request to the server and retrieves the data in JSON format by setting accepts header to application/json, text/javascript. This is same as get() method, the only difference is that getJSON() method specifically retrieves JSON data whereas get() method retrieves any type of data. It is like shortcut method to retrieve JSON data.

Syntax

```
$.getJSON(url,[data],[callback]);
```

Parameter Description:

- Url: request url from which you want to retrieve the data.

- Data: JSON data to be sent to the server as a query string.

- Callback: function to be executed when request succeeds.

The following example shows how to retrieve JSON data using getJSON() method.

Example: jQuery getJSON() Method.

$.getJSON('/jquery/getjsondata', {name:'Steve'}, function (data, textStatus, jqXHR){

$('p').append(data.firstName);

});

<p></p>

In the above example, first parameter is a url from which we want to get JSON data. This can be a web service or any other url that returns JSON data.

The second parameter is data to pass as query string with the GET request. So now, the request url would look like http://mydomain.com/jquery/getjsondata?name=Steve

The third parameter is a callback function which will be executed when request succeeds. The data parameter will be in the JSON format because getJson() method automatically converts server response into a JSON object.

You can attach fail and done callback methods to getJson() method as shown below.

Example: getJSON() Method.

```
$.getJSON('/jquery/getjsondata',  { name:'Steve'},  function(data, textStatus,
jqXHR){

            alert(data.firstName);

      })

      .done(function () { alert('Request done!'); })

      .fail(function (jqxhr,settings,ex) { alert('failed, '+ ex); });
```

The jQuery getScript() Method

The jQuery getScript() method sends http GET request to the server, retrieves the JavaScript file and then executes it. Internally, jQuery getScript() method calls get() method and sets dataType to script.

Syntax

```
$.getScript(url, [callback]);
```

Parameter Description:

- Url: request url from which you want to download JavaScript file.
- Callback: function to be executed when request succeeds.

The following example shows how to download script file using getScript() method.

Example: jQuery getScript() Method.

```
$.getScript('/Scripts/myJavaScriptFile.js', function(script,status,jqxhr){
        alert(status);
    });
```

The jQuery post() Method

The jQuery post() method sends asynchronous http POST request to the server to submit the data to the server and get the response.

Syntax

```
$.post(url,[data],[callback],[type]);
```

Parameter Description:

- Url: request url from which you want to submit & retrieve the data.
- Data: json data to be sent to the server with request as a form data.
- Callback: function to be executed when request succeeds.
- Type: data type of the response content.

Let's see how to submit data and get the response using post() method. Consider the following example.

Example: jQuery post() Method.

```
$.post('/jquery/submitData',   // url
        { myData: 'This is my data.' }, // data to be submit
        function(data, status, jqXHR) {// success callback
```

```
        $('p').append('status: ' + status + ', data: ' + data);

    })
```

```
<p></p>
```

In the above example, first parameter is a url to which we want to send http POST request and submit the data.

The second parameter is a data to submit in JSON format, where key is the name of a parameter and value is the value of parameter.

The third parameter is a success callback function that will be called when request succeeds. The callback function can have three parameters; data, status and jqXHR. The data parameter is a response coming from the server.

The following example shows how to submit and retrieve JSON data using post() method.

Example: submit JSON Data using post() Method.

```
$.post('/submitJSONData',   // url
        { myData: 'This is my data.' }, // data to be submit
        function(data, status, xhr) {    // success callback function
                alert('status: ' + status + ', data: ' + data.responseData);
            },
        'json'); // response data format
```

In the above example, please notice that last parameter is a type of response data. We will get JSON data as a server response. So post() method will automatically parse response into JSON object. Rest of the parameters are same as first example.

You can also attach fail and done callback methods to post() method as shown below.

Example: jQuery post() Method.

```
$.post('/jquery/submitData',
        { myData: 'This is my data.' },
        function(data, status, xhr) {

            $('p').append('status: ' + status + ', data: ' + data);

        }).done(function() { alert('Request done!'); })
        .fail(function(jqxhr, settings, ex) { alert('failed, ' + ex); });
```

```
<p></p>
```

The jQuery Load() Method

The jQuery load() method allows HTML or text content to be loaded from a server and added into a DOM element.

Syntax

```
$.load(url,[data],[callback]);
```

Parameters Description:

- Url: request url from which you want to retrieve the content.
- Data: JSON data to be sent with request to the server.
- Callback: function to be executed when request succeeds.

The following example shows how to load html content from the server and add it to div element.

Example: Load HTML Content.

```
$('#msgDiv').load('/demo.html');
```

```
<div id="msgDiv"></div>
```

In the above example, we have specified html file to load from the server and add its content to the div element.

Note : If no element is matched by the selector then Ajax request will not be sent.

The load() method allows us to specify a portion of the response document to be inserted into DOM element. This can be achieved using url parameter, by specifying selector with url separated by one or multiple space characters as shown in the following example.

Example: jQuery load() Method.

```
$('#msgDiv').load('/demo.html #myHtmlContent');
```

```
<div id="msgDiv"></div>
```

In the above example, content of the element whose id is myHtmlContent, will be added into msgDiv element. The following is a demo.html.

demo.html content:

```
<!DOCTYPE html>

<html xmlns="http://www.w3.org/1999/xhtml">

<head>

    <title></title>
```

```
</head>
<body>
    <h1>This is demo html page.</h1>
    <div id="myHtmlContent">This is my html content.</div>
</body>
</html>
```

The load() method also allows us to specify data to be sent to the server and fetch the data.

Example: Set Data in load().

```
$('#msgDiv').load('getData', // url
                { name: 'bill' },    // data
                function(data, status, jqXGR) {  // callback function
                        alert('data loaded')
                });


<div id="msgDiv"></div>
```

In the above example, first parameter is a url from which we want to fetch the resources. The second parameter is data to be sent to the server. The third parameter is a callback function to execute when request succeeds.

References

- What-is-javascript: edureka.co, Retrieved 11 April, 2019

- Javascript-overview, javascript: tutorialspoint.com, Retrieved 13 August, 2019

- Angularjs-introduction: guru99.com, Retrieved 19 February, 2019

- Angularjs-overview, angularjs: tutorialspoint.com, Retrieved 2 July, 2019

- Reactjs-state, reactjs: tutorialspoint.com, Retrieved 18 February, 2019

- What-and-why-reactjs: c-sharpcorner.com, Retrieved 8 May, 2019

- What-is-meteorjs: educba.com, Retrieved 9 January, 2019

- What-is-Meteor-JS-and-Its-Features: pitechnologies.org, Retrieved 15 March, 2019

- What-is-meteorjs: educba.com, Retrieved 17 January, 2019

- What-is-jquery, jquery: tutorialsteacher.com, Retrieved 27 June, 2019

- Prototypes-in-javascript-5bba2990e04b, better-programming: medium.com, Retrieved 3 March, 2019

Python

Python is the name of a high-level, interpreted, general-purpose programming language. Its design philosophy stresses on code readability. Some of the common python GUI frameworks are PyQt, Tkinter and PyGtk. The chapter closely examines these key frameworks of Python as well as its advantages to provide an extensive understanding of the subject.

Python is an interpreter, object-oriented programming language similar to PERL that has gained popularity because of its clear syntax and readability. Python is said to be relatively easy to learn and portable, meaning its statements can be interpreted in a number of operating systems, including UNIX-based systems, Mac OS, MS-DOS, OS/2, and various versions of Microsoft Windows 98. The source code is freely available and open for modification and reuse. Python has a significant number of users.

A notable feature of Python is its indenting of source statements to make the code easier to read. Python offers dynamic data type, ready-made class, and interfaces to many system calls and libraries. It can be extended, using the C or C++ language.

Python can be used as the script in Microsoft's Active Server Page (ASP) technology. The scoreboard system for the Melbourne (Australia) Cricket Ground is written in Python. Z Object Publishing Environment, a popular web application server, is also written in the Python language.

Advantages of Python

Readable and Maintainable Code

While writing a software application, you must focus on the quality of its source code to simplify maintenance and updates. The syntax rules of Python allow you to express concepts without writing additional code. At the same time, Python, unlike other programming languages, emphasizes on code readability, and allows you to use English keywords instead of punctuations. Hence, you can use Python to build custom applications without writing additional code. The readable and clean code base will help you to maintain and update the software without putting extra time and effort.

Multiple Programming Paradigms

Like other modern programming languages, Python also supports several programming paradigm. It supports object oriented and structured programming fully. Also, its language features support various concepts in functional and aspect-oriented programming. At the same time, Python also features a dynamic type system and automatic memory management. The programming paradigms and language features help you to use Python for developing large and complex software applications.

Compatible with Major Platforms and Systems

At present, Python is supports many operating systems. You can even use Python interpreters to run the code on specific platforms and tools. Also, Python is an interpreted programming language. It allows you to you to run the same code on multiple platforms without recompilation. Hence, you are not required to recompile the code after making any alteration. You can run the modified application code without recompiling and check the impact of changes made to the code immediately. The feature makes it easier for you to make changes to the code without increasing development time.

Robust Standard Library

Its large and robust standard library makes Python score over other programming languages. The standard library allows you to choose from a wide range of modules according to your precise needs. Each module further enables you to add functionality to the Python application without writing additional code. For instance, while writing a web application in Python, you can use specific modules to implement web services, perform string operations, manage operating system interface or work with internet protocols.

Many Open Source Frameworks and Tools

As an open source programming language, Python helps you to curtail software development cost significantly. You can even use several open source Python frameworks, libraries and development tools to curtail development time without increasing development cost. You even have option to choose from a wide range of open source Python frameworks and development tools according to your precise needs. For instance, you can simplify and speedup web application development by using robust Python web frameworks like Django, Flask, Pyramid, Bottle and Cherrypy. Likewise, you can accelerate desktop GUI application development using Python GUI frameworks and toolkits like PyQT, PyJs, PyGUI, Kivy, PyGTK and WxPython.

Simplify Complex Software Development

Python is a general purpose programming language. Hence, you can use the programming language for developing both desktop and web applications. Also, you can use Python for developing complex scientific and numeric applications. Python is designed with features to facilitate data analysis and visualization. You can take advantage of the data analysis features of Python to create custom big data solutions without putting extra time and effort. At the same time, the data visualization libraries and APIs provided by Python help you to visualize and present data in a more appealing and effective way. Many Python developers even use Python to accomplish artificial intelligence (AI) and natural language processing tasks.

Adopt Test Driven Development

You can use Python to create prototype of the software application rapidly. Also, you can build the software application directly from the prototype simply by refactoring the Python code. Python even makes it easier for you to perform coding and testing simultaneously by adopting test driven development (TDD) approach. You can easily write the required tests before writing code and use the tests to assess the application code continuously. The tests can also be used for checking if the application meets predefined requirements based on its source code.

Python GUI Frameworks

Python is an interactive programming language and getting started with programming a GUI (Graphical User Interface) framework is not much of a difficult task. Python has a diverse range of options for GUI frameworks. Here are 4 Best Python GUI Frameworks:

PyQt

PyQt is a python binding of the open-source widget-toolkit Qt, which also functions as a cross-platform application development framework. Qt is a popular C++ framework for writing GUI applications for all major desktop, mobile, and embedded platforms (supports Linux, Windows, MacOS, Android, iOS, Raspberry Pi, and more).

Features of PyQT

Here, are important features of PyQt. PyQt consists of more than six hundred classes covering a range of features such as-

- Graphical User Interfaces
- SQL Databases
- Web toolkits
- XML processing
- Networking

These features can be combined to create advanced UIs as well as standalone applications. A lot of major companies across all industries use Qt. Some examples are LG, Mercedes, AMD, Panasonic, Harman, etc.

PyQt Versions

PyQt is available in two editions, PyQt4 and PyQt5. PyQt4 provides glue code for binding 4.x and 5.x versions of the Qt framework while PyQt5 provides a binding for only the 5.x versions. As a result, PyQt5 is not backward compatible with the deprecated modules of the older version.

Need of PyQt

- PyQt brings together the Qt C++ cross-platform application framework and the cross-platform interpreted language Python.
- Qt is more than a GUI toolkit. It includes abstractions of network sockets, threads, Unicode, regular expressions, SQL databases, SVG, OpenGL, XML, a fully functional web browser, a help system, a multimedia framework, as well as a rich collection of GUI widgets.

- Qt classes employ a signal/slot mechanism for communicating between objects that is type safe but loosely coupled making it easy to create re-usable software components.

- Qt also includes Qt Designer, a graphical user interface designer. PyQt is able to generate Python code from Qt Designer. It is also possible to add new GUI controls written in Python to Qt Designer.

- Python is a simple but powerful object-orientated language. Its simplicity makes it easy to learn, but its power means that large and complex applications can be created. Its interpreted nature means that Python programmers are very productive because there is no edit, compile, link and run development cycle.

- Much of Python's power comes from its comprehensive set of extension modules providing a wide variety of functions including HTTP servers, XML parsers, database access, data compression tools and, of course, graphical user interfaces. Extension modules are usually implemented in either Python, C or C++. Using tools such as SIP it is relatively straight forward to create an extension module that encapsulates an existing C or C++ library. Used in this way, Python can then become the glue to create new applications from established libraries.

- PyQt combines all the advantages of Qt and Python. A programmer has all the power of Qt, but is able to exploit it with the simplicity of Python.

Tkinter

Tkinter is actually an inbuilt Python module used to create simple GUI apps. It is the most commonly used module for GUI apps in the Python.

Python provides the standard library Tkinter for creating the graphical user interface for desktop based applications.

Developing desktop based applications with python Tkinter is not a complex task. An empty Tkinter top-level window can be created by using the following steps-

- Import the Tkinter module.

- Create the main application window.

- Add the widgets like labels, buttons, frames, etc. to the window.

- Call the main event loop so that the actions can take place on the user's computer screen.

Example:

```
1. # !/usr/bin/python3
2. from tkinter import *
3. #creating the application main window.
4. top = Tk()
5. #Entering the event main loop
6. top.mainloop()
```

Output:

Tkinter Widgets

There are various widgets like button, canvas, checkbutton, entry, etc. that are used to build the python GUI applications.

S.no.	Widget	Description
1	Button	The Button is used to add various kinds of buttons to the python application.
2	Canvas	The canvas widget is used to draw the canvas on the window.
3	Checkbutton	The Checkbutton is used to display the CheckButton on the window.
4	Entry	The entry widget is used to display the single-line text field to the user. It is commonly used to accept user values.
5	Frame	It can be defined as a container to which, another widget can be added and organized.
6	Label	A label is a text used to display some message or information about the other widgets.
7	ListBox	The ListBox widget is used to display a list of options to the user.
8	Menubutton	The Menubutton is used to display the menu items to the user.
9	Menu	It is used to add menu items to the user.
10	Message	The Message widget is used to display the message-box to the user.
11	Radiobutton	The Radiobutton is different from a checkbutton. Here, the user is provided with various options and the user can select only one option among them.
12	Scale	It is used to provide the slider to the user.
13	Scrollbar	It provides the scrollbar to the user so that the user can scroll the window up and down.
14	Text	It is different from Entry because it provides a multi-line text field to the user so that the user can write the text and edit the text inside it.
14	Toplevel	It is used to create a separate window container.
15	Spinbox	It is an entry widget used to select from options of values.
16	PanedWindow	It is like a container widget that contains horizontal or vertical panes.
17	LabelFrame	A LabelFrame is a container widget that acts as the container
18	MessageBox	This module is used to display the message-box in the desktop based applications.

Python Tkinter Geometry

The Tkinter geometry specifies the method by using which, the widgets are represented on display.

The python Tkinter provides the following geometry methods:

1. The pack() method

2. The grid() method

3. The place() method

Python Tkinter pack() method

The pack() widget is used to organize widget in the block. The positions widgets added to the python application using the pack() method can be controlled by using the various options specified in the method call.

However, the controls are less and widgets are generally added in the less organized manner.

The syntax to use the pack() is given below.

Syntax

Widget.pack(options) –

A list of possible options that can be passed in pack() is given below:

- Expand: If the expand is set to true, the widget expands to fill any space.

- Fill: By default, the fill is set to NONE. However, we can set it to X or Y to determine whether the widget contains any extra space.

- Size: it represents the side of the parent to which the widget is to be placed on the window.

Example:

```
1. # !/usr/bin/python3
2. from tkinter import *
3. parent = Tk()
4. redbutton = Button(parent, text = "Red", fg = "red")
5. redbutton.pack( side = LEFT)
6. greenbutton = Button(parent, text = "Black", fg = "black")
7. greenbutton.pack( side = RIGHT )
8. bluebutton = Button(parent, text = "Blue", fg = "blue")
9. bluebutton.pack( side = TOP )
10.blackbutton = Button(parent, text = "Green", fg = "red")
11.blackbutton.pack( side = BOTTOM)
12.parent.mainloop()
```

Output:

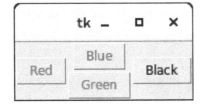

Python Tkinter Grid() Method

The grid() geometry manager organizes the widgets in the tabular form. We can specify the rows and columns as the options in the method call. We can also specify the column span (width) or rowspan(height) of a widget.

This is a more organized way to place the widgets to the python application. The syntax to use the grid() is given below.

Syntax

Widget.grid(options) –

A list of possible options that can be passed inside the grid() method is given below:

- Column: The column number in which the widget is to be placed. The leftmost column is represented by 0.

- Columnspan: The width of the widget. It represents the number of columns up to which, the column is expanded.

- Ipadx, ipady: It represents the number of pixels to pad the widget inside the widget's border.

- Padx, pady: It represents the number of pixels to pad the widget outside the widget's border.

- Row: The row number in which the widget is to be placed. The topmost row is represented by 0.

- Rowspan: The height of the widget, i.e. the number of the row up to which the widget is expanded.

- Sticky: If the cell is larger than a widget, then sticky is used to specify the position of the widget inside the cell. It may be the concatenation of the sticky letters representing the position of the widget. It may be N, E, W, S, NE, NW, NS, EW, ES.

Example:

```
1.  # !/usr/bin/python3
2.  from tkinter import *
3.  parent = Tk()
4.  name = Label(parent,text = "Name").grid(row = 0, column = 0)
5.  e1 = Entry(parent).grid(row = 0, column = 1)
6.  password = Label(parent,text = "Password").grid(row = 1, column = 0)
7.  e2 = Entry(parent).grid(row = 1, column = 1)
8.  submit = Button(parent, text = "Submit").grid(row = 4, column = 0)
9.  parent.mainloop()
```

Output:

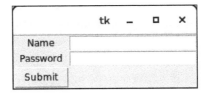

Python Tkinter place() Method

The place() geometry manager organizes the widgets to the specific x and y coordinates.

Syntax

Widget.place(options) –

A list of possible options is given below:

- Anchor: It represents the exact position of the widget within the container. The default value (direction) is NW (the upper left corner).

- Bordermode: The default value of the border type is inside that refers to ignore the parent's inside the border. The other option is outside.

- Height, width: It refers to the height and width in pixels.

- Relheight, relwidth: It is represented as the float between 0.0 and 1.0 indicating the fraction of the parent's height and width.

- Relx, rely: It is represented as the float between 0.0 and 1.0 that is the offset in the horizontal and vertical direction.

- X, y: It refers to the horizontal and vertical offset in the pixels.

Example:

```
1.  # !/usr/bin/python3
2.  from tkinter import *
3.  top = Tk()
4.  top.geometry("400x250")
5.  name = Label(top, text = "Name").place(x = 30,y = 50)
6.  email = Label(top, text = "Email").place(x = 30, y = 90)
7.  password = Label(top, text = "Password").place(x = 30, y = 130)
8.  e1 = Entry(top).place(x = 80, y = 50)
9.  e2 = Entry(top).place(x = 80, y = 90)
10.     e3 = Entry(top).place(x = 95, y = 130)
11.     top.mainloop()
```

Output:

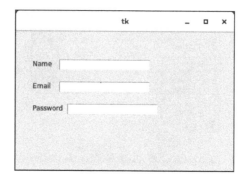

PyGtk

PyGTK is a set of wrappers written in Python and C for GTK + GUI library. It is part of the GNOME project. It offers comprehensive tools for building desktop applications in Python. Python bindings for other popular GUI libraries are also available.

PyQt is a Python port of QT library. Similarly, wxPython toolkit is Python binding for wxWidgets, another popular cross-platform GUI library.

GTK+, or the GIMP Toolkit, is a multi-platform toolkit for creating graphical user interfaces. Offering a complete set of widgets, GTK+ is suitable for projects ranging from small one-off tools to complete application suites.

GTK+ has been designed from the ground up to support a wide range of languages. PyGTK is a Python wrapper for GTK+.

GTK+ is built around the following four libraries –

- Glib – A low-level core library that forms the basis of GTK+. It provides data structure handling for C.

- Pango – A library for layout and rendering of text with an emphasis on internationalization.

- Cairo – A library for 2D graphics with support for multiple output devices (including the X Window System, Win32).

- ATK – A library for a set of interfaces providing accessibility tools such as screen readers, magnifiers, and alternative input devices.

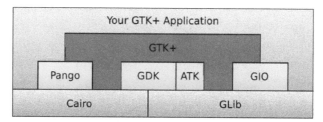

PyGTK eases the process and helps you create programs with a graphical user interface using the Python programming language. The underlying GTK+ library provides all kinds of visual elements and utilities for it to develop full-featured applications for the GNOME Desktop. PyGTK is a cross-platform library. It is free software distributed under the LGPL license.

PyGTK is built around GTK + 2.x. In order to build applications for GTK +3, PyGObject bindings are also available.

Python Variable

A Python variable is a reserved memory location to store values. In other words, a variable in a python program gives data to the computer for processing.

Every value in Python has a datatype. Different data types in python are numbers, list, tuple, strings, dictionary, etc. Variables can be declared by any name or even alphabets like a, aa, abc, etc.

Declaring and using a Variable

Let see an example. We will declare variable "a" and print it.

```
a=100
```

```
print a
```

Re-declare a Variable

You can re-declare the variable even after you have declared it once.

Here we have variable initialized to f=0.

Later, we re-assign the variable f to value "guru99"

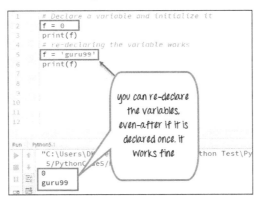

Python 2 Example:

```
# Declare a variable and initialize it
```

```
f = 0
```

```
print f
```

```
# re-declaring the variable works

f = 'guru99'

print f
```

Python 3 Example:

```
# Declare a variable and initialize it

f = 0

print(f)

# re-declaring the variable works

f = 'guru99'

print(f)
```

Concatenate Variables

Let's see whether you can concatenate different data types like string and number together. For example, we will concatenate "Guru" with the number "99".

Unlike Java, which concatenates number with string without declaring number as string, Python requires declaring the number as string otherwise it will show a TypeError.

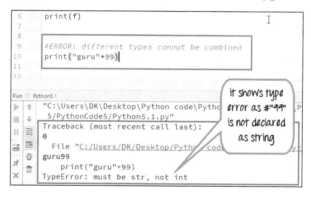

For the following code, you will get undefined output –

```
a="Guru"

b = 99

print a+b
```

Once the integer is declared as string, it can concatenate both "Guru" + str("99")= "Guru99" in the output.

```
a="Guru"

b = 99

print(a+str(b))
```

Local and Global Variables

In Python when you want to use the same variable for rest of your program or module you declare it a global variable, while if you want to use the variable in a specific function or method, you use a local variable.

Let's understand this difference between local and global variable with the below program:

1. Variable "f" is global in scope and is assigned value 101 which is printed in output.

2. Variable f is again declared in function and assumes local scope. It is assigned value "I am learning Python." which is printed out as an output. This variable is different from the global variable "f" define earlier.

3. Once the function call is over, the local variable f is destroyed. At line 12, when we again, print the value of "f" is it displays the value of global variable f=101.

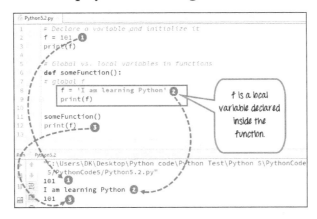

Python 2 Example:

```python
# Declare a variable and initialize it

f = 101

print f

# Global vs. local variables in functions

def someFunction():

# global f

    f = 'I am learning Python'

    print f

someFunction()

print f
```

Python 3 Example:

```python
# Declare a variable and initialize it
```

```
f = 101
print(f)
# Global vs. local variables in functions
def someFunction():
# global f
    f = 'I am learning Python'
    print(f)
someFunction()
print(f)
```

Using the keyword global, you can reference the global variable inside a function:

1. Variable "f" is global in scope and is assigned value 101 which is printed in output.

2. Variable f is declared using the keyword global. This is NOT a local variable, but the same global variable declared earlier. Hence when we print its value, the output is 101.

3. We changed the value of "f" inside the function. Once the function call is over, the changed value of the variable "f" persists. At line 12, when we again, print the value of "f" is it displays the value "changing global variable".

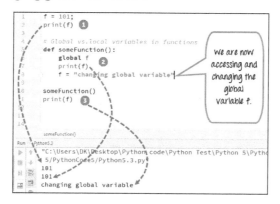

Python 2 Example:

```
f = 101;
print f
# Global vs.local variables in functions
def someFunction():
  global f
  print f
  f = "changing global variable"
someFunction()
print f
```

Python 3 Example:

```
f = 101;

print(f)

# Global vs.local variables in functions

def someFunction():

  global f

  print(f)

  f = "changing global variable"

someFunction()

print(f)
```

Delete a Variable

You can also delete variable using the command del "variable name".

In the example below, we deleted variable f, and when we proceed to print it, we get error "variable name is not defined" which means you have deleted the variable.

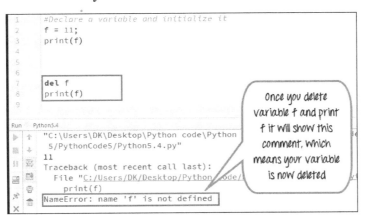

```
f = 11;

print(f)

del f

print(f)
```

Python Data Types

Variables can hold values of different data types. Python is a dynamically typed language hence we need not define the type of the variable while declaring it. The interpreter implicitly binds the value with its type.

Python enables us to check the type of the variable used in the program. Python provides us the type() function which returns the type of the variable passed.

Consider the following example to define the values of different data types and checking its type.

```
A=10
b="Hi Python"
c = 10.5
print(type(a));
print(type(b));
print(type(c));
```

Output:

```
<type 'int'>
<type 'str'>
<type 'float'>
```

Standard Data Types

A variable can hold different types of values. For example, a person's name must be stored as a string whereas its id must be stored as an integer.

Python provides various standard data types that define the storage method on each of them. The data types defined in Python are given below:

1. Numbers
2. String
3. List
4. Tuple
5. Dictionary

Numbers

Number stores numeric values. Python creates Number objects when a number is assigned to a variable. For example;

```
a = 3 , b = 5   #a and b are number objects
```

Python supports 4 types of numeric data.

1. Int (signed integers like 10, 2, 29, etc.)
2. Long (long integers used for a higher range of values like 908090800L, -0x1929292L, etc.)

3. Float (float is used to store floating point numbers like 1.9, 9.902, 15.2, etc.)

4. Complex (complex numbers like 2.14j, 2.0 + 2.3j, etc.)

Python allows us to use a lower-case L to be used with long integers. However, we must always use an upper-case L to avoid confusion.

A complex number contains an ordered pair, i.e., x + iy where x and y denote the real and imaginary parts respectively.

String

The string can be defined as the sequence of characters represented in the quotation marks. In python, we can use single, double, or triple quotes to define a string.

String handling in python is a straightforward task since there are various inbuilt functions and operators provided.

In the case of string handling, the operator + is used to concatenate two strings as the operation "hello"+" python" returns "hello python".

The operator * is known as repetition operator as the operation "Python " *2 returns "Python Python ".

The following example illustrates the string handling in python.

```
1. str1 = 'hello javatpoint' #string str1
2. str2 = ' how are you' #string str2
3. print (str1[0:2]) #printing first two character using slice operator
4. print (str1[4]) #printing 4th character of the string
5. print (str1*2) #printing the string twice
6. print (str1 + str2) #printing the concatenation of str1 and str2
```

Output:

```
he

o

hello javatpointhello javatpoint
hello javatpoint how are you
```

List

Lists are similar to arrays in C. However; the list can contain data of different types. The items stored in the list are separated with a comma (,) and enclosed within square brackets [].

We can use slice [:] operators to access the data of the list. The concatenation operator (+) and repetition operator (*) works with the list in the same way as they were working with the strings.

Consider the following example-

```
1. l  = [1, "hi", "python", 2]
2. print (l[3:]);
3. print (l[0:2]);
4. print (l);
5. print (l + l);
6. print (l * 3);
```

Output:

```
[2]

[1, 'hi']

[1, 'hi', 'python', 2]

[1, 'hi', 'python', 2, 1, 'hi', 'python', 2]

[1, 'hi', 'python', 2, 1, 'hi', 'python', 2, 1, 'hi', 'python', 2]
```

Tuple

A tuple is similar to the list in many ways. Like lists, tuples also contain the collection of the items of different data types. The items of the tuple are separated with a comma (,) and enclosed in parentheses ().

A tuple is a read-only data structure as we can't modify the size and value of the items of a tuple.

Let's see a simple example of the tuple.

```
1. t  = ("hi", "python", 2)
2. print (t[1:]);
3. print (t[0:1]);
4. print (t);
5. print (t + t);
6. print (t * 3);
7. print (type(t))
8. t[2] = "hi";
```

Output:

```
('python', 2)

('hi',)

('hi', 'python', 2)

('hi', 'python', 2, 'hi', 'python', 2)
```

```
('hi', 'python', 2, 'hi', 'python', 2, 'hi', 'python', 2)
<type 'tuple'>
Traceback (most recent call last):
  File "main.py", line 8, in <module>
    t[2] = "hi";
TypeError: 'tuple' object does not support item assignment
```

Dictionary

Dictionary is an ordered set of a key-value pair of items. It is like an associative array or a hash table where each key stores a specific value. Key can hold any primitive data type whereas value is an arbitrary Python object.

The items in the dictionary are separated with the comma and enclosed in the curly braces {}.

Consider the following example-

```
1. d = {1:'Jimmy', 2:'Alex', 3:'john', 4:'mike'};
2. print("1st name is "+d[1]);
3. print("2nd name is "+ d[4]);
4. print (d);
5. print (d.keys());
6. print (d.values());
```

Output:

```
1st name is Jimmy
2nd name is mike
{1: 'Jimmy', 2: 'Alex', 3: 'john', 4: 'mike'}
[1, 2, 3, 4]
['Jimmy', 'Alex', 'john', 'mike']
```

Python Syntax

The syntax of the Python programming language is the set of rules which defines how a Python program will be written.

Python Line Structure

A Python program is divided into a number of logical lines and every logical line is terminated by the token newline. A logical line is created from one or more physical lines.

A line contains only spaces, tabs, form feeds possibly a comment, is known as a blank line, and Python interpreter ignores it.

A physical line is a sequence of characters terminated by an end-of-line sequence (in windows it is called CR LF or return followed by a linefeed and in Unix, it is called LF or linefeed).

```
7% python-syntax-test - E:/python-programs/python-syntax-test
File  Edit  Format  Run  Options  Windows  Help
x = 1
if x>0:
    print("These three lines are Physical/Logical Lines")

|

                                                    Ln: 5 Col: 0
```

Comments in Python

A comment begins with a hash character (#) which is not a part of the string literal and ends at the end of the physical line. All characters after the # character up to the end of the line are part of the comment and the Python interpreter ignores them. It should be noted that Python has no multi-lines or block comments facility.

```
7% python-syntax-test - E:/python-programs/python-syntax-test
File  Edit  Format  Run  Options  Windows  Help
x = 1
#The initial value of x is 1.
if x>0:
    print("These are two comments")  #Print a string.



                                                    Ln: 3 Col: 0
```

Joining Two Lines

When you want to write a long code in a single line you can break the logical line in two or more physical lines using backslash character(\). Therefore when a physical line ends with a backslash characters(\) and not a part of a string literal or comment then it can join another physical line.

```
7% python-syntax-test - E:/python-programs/python-syntax-test
File  Edit  Format  Run  Options  Windows  Help
u = 0
v = 1
w = 2
x = 3
y = 4
z = 5

if u==0 and v>0 \
   and w>1 and x>2 \
   and y>3 and z>4:
    print("This is an example of line joining.")


                                                    Ln: 6 Col: 5
```

Multiple Statements on a Single Line

You can write two separate statements into a single line using a semicolon (;) character between two line.

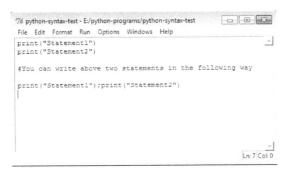

Indentation

Python uses whitespace (spaces and tabs) to define program blocks whereas other languages like C, C++ use braces ({}) to indicate blocks of codes for class, functions or flow control. The number of whitespaces (spaces and tabs) in the indentation is not fixed, but all statements within the block must be the indented same amount. In the following program, the block statements have no indentation.

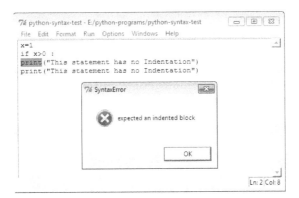

This is a program with single space indentation.

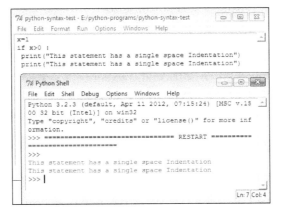

This is a program with single tab indentation.

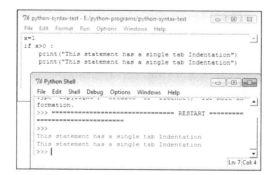

Here is an another program with an indentation of a single space + a single tab.

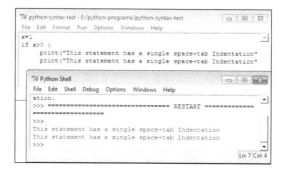

Python Coding Style

- Use 4 spaces per indentation and no tabs.

- Do not mix tabs and spaces. Tabs create confusion and it is recommended to use only spaces.

- Maximum line length: 79 characters which help users with a small display.

- Use blank lines to separate top-level function and class definitions and single blank line to separate methods definitions inside a class and larger blocks of code inside functions.

- When possible, put inline comments (should be complete sentences).

- Use spaces around expressions and statements.

Python if-elif-else

The if-elif-else statement is used to conditionally execute a statement or a block of statements. Conditions can be true or false, execute one thing when the condition is true, something else when the condition is false.

The Python if Statement

The Python if statement is same as it is with other programming languages. It executes a set of statements conditionally, based on the value of a logical expression.

Here is the general form of a one way if statement.

Syntax

```
if expression :

    statement_1

    statement_2

    ....
```

In the above case, expression specifies the conditions which are based on Boolean expression. When a Boolean expression is evaluated it produces either a value of true or false. If the expression evaluates true the same amount of indented statement(s) following if will be executed. This group of the statement(s) is called a block.

Python if-else Statement

In Python if-else statement, if has two blocks, one following the expression and other following the else clause. Here is the syntax.

Syntax

```
if expression :

    statement_1

    statement_2

    ....

     else :

    statement_3

    statement_4

    ....
```

In the above case if the expression evaluates to true the same amount of indented statements(s) following if will be executed and if the expression evaluates to false the same amount of indented statements(s) following else will be executed. See the following example. The program will print the second print statement as the value of a is 10.

```
a=10

if(a>10):

    print("Value of a is greater than 10")

else :

    print("Value of a is 10")
```

Output:

```
Value of a is 10
```

Flowchart

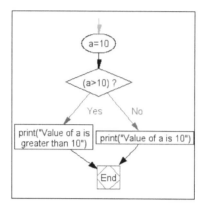

Python if-elif-else Statement

Sometimes a situation arises when there are several conditions. To handle the situation Python allows adding any number of elif clause after an if and before an else clause. Here is the syntax.

Syntax

```
if expression1 :

        statement_1

        statement_2

        ....


    elif expression2 :

    statement_3

    statement_4

    ....

    elif expression3 :

    statement_5

    statement_6

    .................

    else :

    statement_7

    statement_8
```

In the above case Python evaluates each expression (i.e. the condition) one by one and if a true condition is found the statement(s) block under that expression will be executed. If no true condition is found the statement(s) block under else will be executed. In the following example, we have applied if, series of elif and else to get the type of a variable.

```python
var1 = 1+2j
if (type(var1) == int):
    print("Type of the variable is Integer")
elif (type(var1) == float):
    print("Type of the variable is Float")
elif (type(var1) == complex):
    print("Type of the variable is Complex")
elif (type(var1) == bool):
    print("Type of the variable is Bool")
elif (type(var1) == str):
    print("Type of the variable is String")
elif (type(var1) == tuple):
    print("Type of the variable is Tuple")
elif (type(var1) == dict):
    print("Type of the variable is Dictionaries")
elif (type(var1) == list):
    print("Type of the variable is List")
else:
    print("Type of the variable is Unknown")
```

Output:

```
Type of the variable is Complex
```

Flowchart

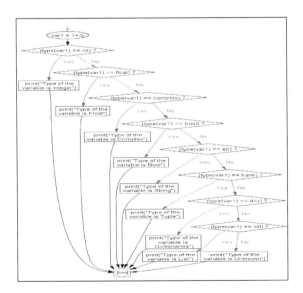

Nested if-else Statement

In general nested if-else statement is used when we want to check more than one conditions. Conditions are executed from top to bottom and check each condition whether it evaluates to true or not. If a true condition is found the statement(s) block associated with the condition executes otherwise it goes to next condition.

Syntax

Here is the syntax:

```
if expression1 :

        if expression2 :

          statement_3

          statement_4

      ....

    else :

        statement_5

        statement_6

      ....

    else :

        statement_7

      statement_8
```

In the above syntax expression1 is checked first, if it evaluates to true then the program control goes to next if - else part otherwise it goes to the last else statement and executes statement_7, statement_8 etc. Within the if - else if expression2 evaluates true then statement_3, statement_4 will execute otherwise statement_5, statement_6 will execute. See the following example.

```
age = 38

if (age >= 11):

  print ("You are eligible to see the Football match.")

  if (age <= 20 or age >= 60):

      print("Ticket price is $12")

  else:

      print("Tic kit price is $20")

else:

    print ("You're not eligible to buy a ticket.")
```

Output:

```
You are eligible to see the Football match.

Tic kit price is $20
```

In the above example age is set to 38, therefore the first expression (age >= 11) evaluates to True and the associated print statement prints the string "You are eligible to see the Football match". There after program control goes to next if statement and the condition (38 is outside <=20 or >=60) is matched and prints "Tic kit price is $12".

Flowchart

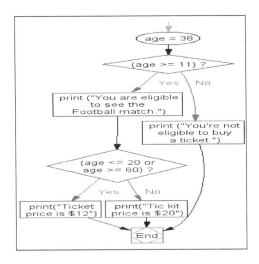

Use the and Operator in an if Statement

```
#create two boolean objects

x = False

y = True


#The validation will be True only if all the expressions generate a value True
if x and y:
    print('Both x and y are True')
else:
    print('x is False or y is False or both x and y are False')
```

Output:

```
x is False or y is False or both x and y are False
```

Use the in Operator in an if Statement

```
#create a string
```

```
s = 'jQuery'

#create a list

l = ['JavaScript', 'jQuery', 'ZinoUI']


# in operator is used to replace various expressions that use the or operator

if s in l:

    print(s + 'Tutorial')


#Alternate if statement with or operator


if s == 'JavaScript' or s == 'jQuery' or s == 'ZinoUI':

    print(s + 'Tutorial')
```

Output:

```
jQuery Tutorial

jQuery Tutorial
```

Write an if-else in a Single Line of Code

```
#create a integer

n = 150

print(n)


#if n is greater than 500, n is multiplied by 7, otherwise n is divided by 7

result = n * 7 if n > 500 else n / 7

print(result)
```

Output:

```
150

21.428571428571427
```

Define a Negative if

If a condition is true the not operator is used to reverse the logical state, then logical not operator will make it false.

```
#create a integer
```

```
x = 20
print(x)


#uses the not operator to reverse the result of the logical expression


if not x == 50:
    print('the value of x different from 50')
else:
    print('the value of x is equal to 50')
```

Output:

```
20
 the value of x different from 50
```

Python for Loop

Like most other languages, Python has for loops, but it differs a bit from other like C or Pascal. In Python for loop is used to iterate over the items of any sequence including the Python list, string, tuple etc. The for loop is also used to access elements from a container (for example list, string, tuple) using built-in function range().

Syntax

```
for variable_name in sequence:
    statement_1
    statement_2
    ....
```

Parameter

Name	Description
variable_name	It indicates target variable which will set a new value for each iteration of the loop.
sequence	A sequence of values that will be assigned to the target variable variable_name. Values are provided using a list or a string or from the built-in function range().
statement_1, statement_2	Block of program statements.

Example: Python for loop.

```
>>> #The list has four elements, indices start at 0 and end at 3
>>> color_list = ["Red", "Blue", "Green", "Black"]
```

```
>>> for c in color_list:
        print(c)


    Red

    Blue

    Green

    Black

>>>
```

In the above example color_list is a sequence contains a list of various color names. When the for loop executed the first item (i.e. Red) is assigned to the variable c. After this, the print statement will execute and the process will continue until we reach the end of the list.

Python for Loop and Range() Function

The range() function returns a list of consecutive integers. The function has one, two or three parameters where last two parameters are optional. It is widely used in for loops. Here is the syntax.

```
range(a)
```

```
range(a,b)
```

```
range(a,b,c)
```

range(a) : Generates a sequence of numbers from 0 to a, excluding a, incrementing by 1.

Syntax

```
for <variable> in range(<number>):
```

Example:

```
>>> for a in range(4):
    print(a)


    0

    1

    2

    3

>>>
```

range(a,b): Generates a sequence of numbers from a to b excluding b, incrementing by 1.

Syntax

```
for "variable" in range ("start_number", "end_number"):
```

Example:

```
>>> for a in range (2,7):
 print (a)
```

```
2

3

4

5

6
```

```
>>>
```

range(a,b,c): Generates a sequence of numbers from a to b excluding b, incrementing by c.

Example:

```
>>> for a in range (2,19,5):
  print (a)
```

```
2

7

12

17
```

```
>>>
```

Python for Loop: Iterating Over tuple, List and Dictionary

Example: Iterating over tuple.

The following example counts the number of even and odd numbers from a series of numbers-

```
numbers = (1, 2, 3, 4, 5, 6, 7, 8, 9) # Declaring the tuple
count_odd = 0
count_even = 0
for x in numbers:
        if x % 2:
```

```
            count_odd+=1
        else:
            count_even+=1
print("Number of even numbers :",count_even)
print("Number of odd numbers :",count_odd)
```

Output:

```
Number of even numbers:4
Number of odd numbers: 5
```

In the above example a tuple named numbers is declared which holds the integers 1 to 9. The best way to check if a given number is even or odd is to use the modulus operator (%). The operator returns the remainder when dividing two numbers. Modulus of 8 % 2 returns 0 as 8 is divided by 2, therefore 8 is even and modulus of 5 % 2 returns 1 therefore 5 is odd.

The for loop iterates through the tuple and we test modulus of x % 2 is true or not, for every item in the tuple and the process will continue until we rich the end of the tuple. When it is true count_even increase by one otherwise count_odd is increased by one.

Finally, we print the number of even and odd numbers through print statements.

Example: Iterating over list.

In the following example for loop iterates through the list "datalist" and prints each item and its corresponding Python type.

```
datalist = [1452, 11.23, 1+2j, True, 'w3resource', (0, -1), [5, 12],
{"class":'V', "section":'A'}]
for item in datalist:
    print ("Type of ",item, " is ", type(item))
```

Output:

```
Type of  1452  is  <class 'int'>
Type of  11.23  is  <class 'float'>
Type of  (1+2j)  is  <class 'complex'>
Type of  True  is  <class 'bool'>
Type of  w3resource  is  <class 'str'>
Type of  (0, -1)  is  <class 'tuple'>
Type of  [5, 12]  is  <class 'list'>
Type of  {'section': 'A', 'class': 'V'}  is  <class 'dict'>
```

Example: Iterating over dictionary.

In the following example for loop iterates through the dictionary "color" through its keys and prints each key.

```
>>> color = {"c1": "Red", "c2": "Green", "c3": "Orange"}
>>> for key in color:
    print(key)


c2
c1
c3
>>>
```

Following for loop iterates through its values:

```
>>> color = {"c1": "Red", "c2": "Green", "c3": "Orange"}
>>> for value in color.values():
    print(value)


Green
Red
Orange
>>>
```

You can attach an optional else clause with for statement, in this case, syntax will be –

```
for variable_name in sequence :
    statement_1
    statement_2
    . . . .
else :
    statement_3
    statement_4
    . . . .
```

The else clause is only executed after completing the for loop. If a break statement executes in first program block and terminates the loop then the else clause does not execute.

Python While Loop

Loops are used to repeatedly execute a block of program statements. The basic loop structure in Python is while loop. Here is the syntax.

Syntax

While (expression):

    statement_1

    statement_2

    ....

The while loop runs as long as the expression (condition) evaluates to true and execute the program block. The condition is checked every time at the beginning of the loop and the first time when the expression evaluates to false, the loop stops without executing any remaining statement(s). The following example prints the digits 0 to 4 as we set the condition $x < 5$.

```
x = 0;
while (x < 5):
        print(x)
        x += 1
```

Output:

```
0
1
2
3
4
```

One thing we should remember that a while loop tests its condition before the body of the loop (block of program statements) is executed. If the initial test returns false, the body is not executed at all. For example the following code never prints out anything since before executing the condition evaluates to false.

```
x = 10;
while (x < 5):
        print(x)
        x += 1
```

Flowchart

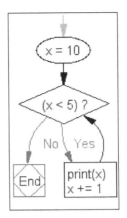

The following while loop is an infinite loop, using True as the condition:

```
x = 10;
while (True):
    print(x)
    x += 1
```

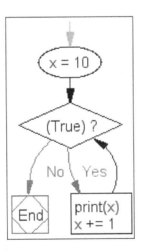

Python: While and Else Statement

There is a structural similarity between while and else statement. Both have a block of statement(s) which is only executed when the condition is true. The difference is that block belongs to if statement executes once whereas block belongs to while statement executes repeatedly.

You can attach an optional else clause with while statement, in this case, syntax will be –

while (expression) :

  statement_1

statement_2

......

else :

statement_3

statement_4

......

The while loop repeatedly tests the expression (condition) and, if it is true, executes the first block of program statements. The else clause is only executed when the condition is false it may be the first time it is tested and will not execute if the loop breaks, or if an exception is raised. If a break statement executes in first program block and terminates the loop then the else clause does not execute. In the following example, while loop calculates the sum of the integers from 0 to 9 and after completing the loop, else statement executes.

```
x = 0;

s = 0

while (x < 10):

    s = s + x

    x = x + 1

else :

    print('The sum of first 9 integers : ',s)
```

Output:

```
The sum of first 9 integers:   45
```

Flowchart

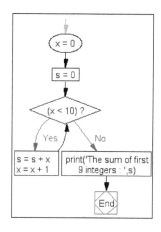

Example: while loop with if-else and break statement.

```
x = 1;
```

```
s = 0
while (x < 10):
    s = s + x
    x = x + 1
    if (x == 5):
        break
else :
    print('The sum of first 9 integers : ',s)
print('The sum of ',x,' numbers is :',s)
```

Output:

```
The sum of  5  numbers is : 10
```

In the above example the loop is terminated when x becomes 5. Here we use break statement to terminate the while loop without completing it, therefore program control goes to outside the while - else structure and execute the next print statement.

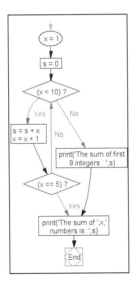

Python Break and Continue Statement

The break statement is used to exit a for or a while loop. The purpose of this statement is to end the execution of the loop (for or while) immediately and the program control goes to the statement after the last statement of the loop. If there is an optional else statement in while or for loop it skips the optional clause also. Here is the syntax.

Syntax

```
while (expression1) :

    statement_1
```

```
    statement_2

    ......

    if expression2 :

    break


for variable_name in sequence :

    statement_1

    statement_2

    if expression3 :

       break
```

Example: break in for loop.

In the following example for loop breaks when the count value is 5. The print statement after the for loop displays the sum of first 5 elements of the tuple numbers.

```
numbers = (1, 2, 3, 4, 5, 6, 7, 8, 9) # Declaring the tuple

num_sum = 0

count = 0

for x in numbers:

    num_sum = num_sum + x

    count = count + 1

    if count == 5:

        break
print ("Sum of first ",count,"integers is: ", num_sum)
```

Output:

```
Sum of first  5 integers is:  15
```

Example: break in while loop.

In the following example while loop breaks when the count value is 5. The print statement after the while loop displays the value of num_sum (i.e. 0+1+2+3+4).

```
num_sum = 0

count = 0

while(count<10) :

    num_sum = num_sum + count
```

```
    count = count + 1
    if count== 5:
        break
print("Sum of first ",count,"integers is: ", num_sum)
```

Output:

```
Sum of first  5 integers is :  10
```

Continue Statement

The continue statement is used in a while or for loop to take the control to the top of the loop without executing the rest statements inside the loop. Here is a simple example.

```
for x in range(7):
    if (x == 3 or x==6):
        continue
    print(x)
```

Output:

```
0
1
2
4
5
```

In the above example, the for loop prints all the numbers from 0 to 6 except 3 and 6 as the continue statement returns the control of the loop to the top.

Python Strings

String Literals

String literals in python are surrounded by either single quotation marks, or double quotation marks.

```
'hello' is the same as "hello".
```

You can display a string literal with the print() function:

Example:

```
print("Hello")

print('Hello')
```

Assign String to a Variable

Assigning a string to a variable is done with the variable name followed by an equal sign and the string.

Example:

```
a = "Hello"
print(a)
```

Multiline Strings

You can assign a multiline string to a variable by using three quotes.

Example:

You can use three double quotes-

```
a = """Lorem ipsum dolor sit amet,
consectetur adipiscing elit,
sed do eiusmod tempor incididunt
ut labore et dolore magna aliqua."""
print(a)
```

Or three single quotes:

Example:

```
a = '''Lorem ipsum dolor sit amet,
consectetur adipiscing elit,
sed do eiusmod tempor incididunt
ut labore et dolore magna aliqua.'''
print(a)
```

In the result, the line breaks are inserted at the same position as in the code.

Strings are Arrays

Like many other popular programming languages, strings in Python are arrays of bytes representing unicode characters.

However, Python does not have a character data type, a single character is simply a string with a length of 1.

Square brackets can be used to access elements of the string.

Example:

Get the character at position 1 (remember that the first character has the position 0);

```
a = "Hello, World!"

print(a[1])
```

Slicing

You can return a range of characters by using the slice syntax.

Specify the start index and the end index, separated by a colon, to return a part of the string.

Example:

Get the characters from position 2 to position 5 (not included):

```
b = "Hello, World!"

print(b[2:5])
```

Negative Indexing

Use negative indexes to start the slice from the end of the string:

Example:

Get the characters from position 5 to position 1, starting the count from the end of the string:

```
b = "Hello, World!"

print(b[-5:-2])
```

String Length

To get the length of a string, use the len() function.

Example:

The len() function returns the length of a string:

```
a = "Hello, World!"

print(len(a))
```

String Methods

Python has a set of built-in methods that you can use on strings.

Example:

The strip() method removes any whitespace from the beginning or the end:

```
a = " Hello, World! "

print(a.strip()) # returns "Hello, World!"
```

Example:

The lower() method returns the string in lower case;

```
a = "Hello, World!"
print(a.lower())
```

Example:

The `upper()` method returns the string in upper case:

```
a = "Hello, World!"
print(a.upper())
```

Example:

The `replace()` method replaces a string with another string:

```
a = "Hello, World!"
print(a.replace("H", "J"))
```

Example:

The `split()` method splits the string into substrings if it finds instances of the separator:

```
a = "Hello, World!"
print(a.split(",")) # returns ['Hello', ' World!']
```

Check String

To check if a certain phrase or character is present in a string, we can use the keywords `in` or `not in`.

Example:

Check if the phrase "ain" is present in the following text:

```
txt = "The rain in Spain stays mainly in the plain"
x = "ain" in txt
print(x)
```

Example:

Check if the phrase "ain" is not present in the following text:

```
txt = "The rain in Spain stays mainly in the plain"
x = "ain" not in txt
print(x)
```

String Concatenation

To concatenate, or combine, two strings you can use the + operator.

Example:

Merge variable a with variable b into variable c:

```
a = "Hello"

b = "World"

c = a + b

print(c)
```

Example:

To add a space between them, add a " ":

```
a = "Hello"

b = "World"

c = a + " " + b

print(c)
```

String Format

Example:

```
age = 36

txt = "My name is John, I am " + age

print(txt)
```

But we can combine strings and numbers by using the format() method!

The format() method takes the passed arguments, formats them, and places them in the string where the placeholders {} are:

Example:

Use the format() method to insert numbers into strings:

```
age = 36

txt = "My name is John, and I am {}"

print(txt.format(age))
```

The format() method takes unlimited number of arguments, and are placed into the respective placeholders:

Example:

```
quantity = 3

itemno = 567
```

```
price = 49.95

myorder = "I want {} pieces of item {} for {} dollars."

print(myorder.format(quantity, itemno, price))
```

You can use index numbers {0} to be sure the arguments are placed in the correct placeholders:

Example:

```
quantity = 3

itemno = 567

price = 49.95

myorder = "I want to pay {2} dollars for {0} pieces of item {1}."

print(myorder.format(quantity, itemno, price))
```

String Methods

Python has a set of built-in methods that you can use on strings.

Note: All string methods returns new values. They do not change the original string.

Method	Description
capitalize()	Converts the first character to upper case
casefold()	Converts string into lower case
center()	Returns a centered string
count()	Returns the number of times a specified value occurs in a string
encode()	Returns an encoded version of the string
endswith()	Returns true if the string ends with the specified value
expandtabs()	Sets the tab size of the string
find()	Searches the string for a specified value and returns the position of where it was found
format()	Formats specified values in a string
format_map()	Formats specified values in a string
index()	Searches the string for a specified value and returns the position of where it was found
isalnum()	Returns True if all characters in the string are alphanumeric
isalpha()	Returns True if all characters in the string are in the alphabet
isdecimal()	Returns True if all characters in the string are decimals
isdigit()	Returns True if all characters in the string are digits
isidentifier()	Returns True if the string is an identifier
islower()	Returns True if all characters in the string are lower case
isnumeric()	Returns True if all characters in the string are numeric
isprintable()	Returns True if all characters in the string are printable
isspace()	Returns True if all characters in the string are whitespaces
istitle()	Returns True if the string follows the rules of a title
isupper()	Returns True if all characters in the string are upper case
join()	Joins the elements of an iterable to the end of the string

ljust()	Returns a left justified version of the string
lower()	Converts a string into lower case
lstrip()	Returns a left trim version of the string
maketrans()	Returns a translation table to be used in translations
partition()	Returns a tuple where the string is parted into three parts
replace()	Returns a string where a specified value is replaced with a specified value
rfind()	Searches the string for a specified value and returns the last position of where it was found
rindex()	Searches the string for a specified value and returns the last position of where it was found
rjust()	Returns a right justified version of the string
rpartition()	Returns a tuple where the string is parted into three parts
rsplit()	Splits the string at the specified separator, and returns a list
rstrip()	Returns a right trim version of the string
split()	Splits the string at the specified separator, and returns a list
splitlines()	Splits the string at line breaks and returns a list
startswith()	Returns true if the string starts with the specified value
strip()	Returns a trimmed version of the string
swapcase()	Swaps cases, lower case becomes upper case and vice versa
title()	Converts the first character of each word to upper case
translate()	Returns a translated string
upper()	Converts a string into upper case
zfill()	Fills the string with a specified number of 0 values at the beginning.

References

- Python: techtarget.com, Retrieved 30 August, 2019

- Python-7-important-reasons-why-you-should-use-python-5801a98a0d0b: medium.com, Retrieved 4 April, 2019

- Pyqt-tutorial: guru99.com, Retrieved 15 March, 2019

- Intro, software: riverbankcomputing.com, Retrieved 18 May, 2019

- Python-tkinter: javatpoint.com, Retrieved 28 January, 2019

- Pygtk-introduction, pygtk: tutorialspoint.com, Retrieved 3 June, 2019

- Variables-in-python: guru99.com, Retrieved 23 May, 2019

- Python-data-types: javatpoint.com, Retrieved 6 February, 2019

- Python-syntax, python: w3resource.com, Retrieved 11 June, 2019

- Python-strings, python: w3schools.com, Retrieved 20 April, 2019

- Python-file-handling, python: w3schools.com, Retrieved 10 July, 2019

Permissions

All chapters in this book are published with permission under the Creative Commons Attribution Share Alike License or equivalent. Every chapter published in this book has been scrutinized by our experts. Their significance has been extensively debated. The topics covered herein carry significant information for a comprehensive understanding. They may even be implemented as practical applications or may be referred to as a beginning point for further studies.

We would like to thank the editorial team for lending their expertise to make the book truly unique. They have played a crucial role in the development of this book. Without their invaluable contributions this book wouldn't have been possible. They have made vital efforts to compile up to date information on the varied aspects of this subject to make this book a valuable addition to the collection of many professionals and students.

This book was conceptualized with the vision of imparting up-to-date and integrated information in this field. To ensure the same, a matchless editorial board was set up. Every individual on the board went through rigorous rounds of assessment to prove their worth. After which they invested a large part of their time researching and compiling the most relevant data for our readers.

The editorial board has been involved in producing this book since its inception. They have spent rigorous hours researching and exploring the diverse topics which have resulted in the successful publishing of this book. They have passed on their knowledge of decades through this book. To expedite this challenging task, the publisher supported the team at every step. A small team of assistant editors was also appointed to further simplify the editing procedure and attain best results for the readers.

Apart from the editorial board, the designing team has also invested a significant amount of their time in understanding the subject and creating the most relevant covers. They scrutinized every image to scout for the most suitable representation of the subject and create an appropriate cover for the book.

The publishing team has been an ardent support to the editorial, designing and production team. Their endless efforts to recruit the best for this project, has resulted in the accomplishment of this book. They are a veteran in the field of academics and their pool of knowledge is as vast as their experience in printing. Their expertise and guidance has proved useful at every step. Their uncompromising quality standards have made this book an exceptional effort. Their encouragement from time to time has been an inspiration for everyone.

The publisher and the editorial board hope that this book will prove to be a valuable piece of knowledge for students, practitioners and scholars across the globe.

Index

CPSIA information can be obtained
at www.ICGtesting.com
Printed in the USA
LVHW061308160222
711210LV00004B/175

9 781647 280246